GOLFGAMES:

THE SIDE GAMES WE PLAY & WAGER

R. M. USSAK

DOGLEG PUBLICATIONS

First Edition   10 9

DESIGN, GRAPHICS, LOGO, and
CARTOON ILLUSTRATIONS by CRAIG A. ARBON

Acknowledgments

Mike Ashurst, who originally planted the seed for the book;
Paul MacDonald, for the advice and constructive
suggestions; Judi Dickerson and Laurie Cowan for the help
and time spent on WordPerfect; the Boys at De Pals, Costa
Brava; Dom "Zeke" Ziccardi, Bill "Cecil" Lindley, Jim "Bart"
Bartlein, who all had games for me to include in the book;
Craig Arbon, partner, whose creativity has enabled us to
provide levity as illustrated by "our" players and cartoons. A
warm and appreciative thanks to all of you, and to the many
others who advised me of the side games they play.

Library of Congress Catalog Number: 91-70352
ISBN 0-9629052-0-8

TABLE OF CONTENTS

An Overview

It's a game that is played by over 50 million people in over 76 countries around the world. It's a game that knows no boundaries, regionally, nationally, or geographically. Whether you are from the North American or South American continent, Europe, Southeast Asia, the continent down under, Australia, or the reputed ancient home of the game, Scotland, the game is immutably the same.

Of course, there are some differences such as the number of sand traps you have to confront, or the number of holes with water that come into play, possibly the fact that you have to play through a veritable forest, or play on a course built in the mountains with so many ups and downs that you think you're a mountain goat, or possibly you are on a course that has rough nothing like your course and is so thick and high that you are lucky to find your ball, much less hit it out of the rough. Was the greens keeper on vacation?

However, despite the changes in topography, vegetation or the scenic sights that you encounter, it's a game that is played with basically the same rules, equipment and intentions. Unfortunately, for most of us those intentions and/or desires are not achieved and, more times than not, the game just does not turn out the way we had dreamed, desired or intended.

That blasted white sphere just didn't go where I wanted it to, didn't break the way I thought it would, or the distance must be wrong! I overshot the green and wound up in heavy rough, or I undershot the green and am now in a sand trap which, for most amateurs dregs up nightmares of past sand play. How about the easy chip shot just off the green which you somehow "miss"? You either skull it over the green into the rough or into the sand trap that wasn't even in your mind as you were about to chip. Or you stub the chip, and you have "hit" it so fat that you're lucky if the ball goes a foot or two, much less gets to the green.

What about that 30-foot putt that's facing you with or without break, and you just didn't have your Wheaties that morning and, as a result, your putt barely gets halfway to the hole. Or on the other hand, you did have your Wheaties that morning and, as a result, your putt goes 15 feet by the hole—what kept that putt out of the hole? Or you just have the hands and touch of a gorilla on a particular day to the point that you are even nervous over the short two- and three-foot putts.

Maybe you are on the tee and have been driving well all day but on this tee shot you "duck" it really bad to the left. Possibly you don't have a swing in which you hook the ball but, instead, you have a swing in which you hit the big banana ball, otherwise known as the "slice." Or possibly you have hit the tee shot so badly you almost whiffed it; however, you did make contact with the top eighth of the ball and dribbled it off the tee—it did go straight, though.

It's a game that you can go out one day and come back another and say either,"How the hell can I shoot that bad after scoring so well previously?" or possibly, "What the hell did I do right? I haven't played that well in a long time."

It's a game that is most frustrating and in which one is bound eventually to hear all sorts of expletives, some of which might even be new. It's a game in which you might be playing with a friend who is usually quite calm, one who never gets angry, but after hitting a real bad shot, starts cursing a blue streak; then you hear whomp—whomp—whomp—whomp, which is sometimes called the helicopter, but more commonly known as the thrown club. It's a game that changes peoples' personalities and demeanors. It's a game that you truly cannot predict. It's a game that keeps us coming back for more of the challenge to do what we want or hope to do with that small white sphere.

However, this game is unlike any other in that there can be a so-called parity among players, and that parity is achieved through utilization of a handicap system based upon scoring versus par. This system basically computes your proficiency or lack thereof determined by the scores that you have shot and how those rounds compare to par. Par is that elevated plateau that tells one that the ball should be struck or putted no more than x number of times before the ball should be in the four-and-one-quarter inch diameter hole in the ground called the cup. If you end up in the cup in less than x you are under par; if you end up in the cup more than x you are over par. The latter probably applies to over 99 percent of all those who play the game.

As a result of this unique system, a whole new world of permutations on how the game can be played has evolved. The traditional medal play for the most part has been supplanted by match play, Nassaus, best balls, high ball/low ball, and many more variations. They all allow players of different levels of proficiency to compete against each other based upon those differences in level of play and, for the most part, based upon handicap. There are of course other forms of play which do not involve handicaps. However, one reason we all keep coming back, besides trying to best that white sphere, is the friendly competition that invariably accompanies a round of play and that, in one form or another, involves wagering.

It can involve just a friendly purchase of a drink for the winner by the loser, or the loser may buy dinner and drinks! Or it can involve a dime a point, a dollar a point, five dollars a side or a dollar a yard per hole. The games that can be played and the stakes or bets vary as much as one's imagination.

That's what this brief book is all about: The games people play and how they play and bet them. As mentioned previously, it is a unique game played throughout the world and one which, for most of us, besides being supposedly relaxing or a source of exercise, is frustrating as hell! It's a game called golf, a simple word that in no way portends what is in store for those who choose to play it. I press!

FOREWORD

It all started for me when I was a youngster and all the experience I had of the game of golf was the small putt-putt courses with those impossible anthill or windmill holes. However, at the age of thirteen my experiences and vocabulary regarding golf were enhanced when I began caddying at a private club.

As a matter of fact, I started caddying when they came out with those huge golf bags that we called kangaroo bags. Those bags at the time were almost as big as I was, and sure enough, when I began caddying, I invariably wound up carrying one of those monstrosities. Unfortunately, for the most part, the golfers with these kangaroo bags played a game that was directly proportional to the size of their bag! At this point I was lucky to just make it through one round of golf, and didn't even dream of carrying two golf bags. Besides, caddying for one person when I didn't know what I was doing was difficult enough.

I did, however, survive those first few weeks of caddying and found out what epsom salts were and how they soothed sore shoulders. I also found out that my shoulders hurt because those kangaroo bags with all those different compartments carried almost everything under the sun, including dozens of golf balls, dozens and dozens of tees, golf gloves (some of which looked and smelled as if they had died and gone to heaven at least twice), bandaids, toothpicks, adhesive tape, spare spikes, ball markers, divot repairers, pencils (some with erasers) and pens, new and old score cards with past claims to fame of previous great rounds of golf or of that unbelievable eagle or double eagle, spare golf shoes, socks, rain gear and umbrellas, a towel, a book or books on USGA golf rules and regulations, Ben-Gay or some type of sun lotion, bug spray, aspirin and often a fifth of booze used to build moral confidence or to ease the pain of missing that one- or two-foot putt! I am sure I have inadvertently left out some item or another, but just thinking about the above, my shoulders are getting sore!

After caddying for about a month I finally became an official caddy and was given a caddy badge indicating that I was now caddy 96. I had survived those first weeks and started to actually think about the time when I would be able to carry two golf bags, known as a double loop. However, before that was to happen, I was indoctrinated into a new world of language which changed the meaning of all types of words I thought I knew. Hooks, duck hooks, slices, banana balls, chilly-dipping, skulling the ball, the yips and the thing called a shank which even sounded ominous, were a few of the words in this new language. Also, there were other things to learn, such as not stepping in someone's line, marking the ball, tending the pin, replacing that divot, repairing a ball mark, raking the trap, and many more.

It was also during my first month of caddying that I heard members talking about a Nassau, which I thought was a reference to that vacation place in the Caribbean. Then I heard them talking about skins, which I thought at the time was a reference to the football team or possibly the skins in a basketball game in which they played against the shirts. When the members started to say things like, "I press you," or "We accept your press," and "Double press you," or "That's two tie all tie and therefore your skin has been nullified," I realized how little I understood of their talk.

I did learn fast, but at the expense of hard-earned money I had made carrying a golf bag around the course. The way I learned was on caddy day (which was always on Mondays when the course was closed to members for course maintenance) when twenty or thirty caddies got together and played golf for the entire day at no cost except for the bets lost to other caddies. This was where I started to play in the

Nassau games, the skin games, and the best ball games, and learned their meanings and how you won or lost. I learned the rules of the game and the variety of games that can be played from the older and more experienced caddies, some of whom were outstanding golfers. When the caddies played they always played the ball down, and with very few exceptions we played the ball as it lay.

In those days, there were some really good golfing caddies and regardless of how well I played, I could never beat them, even if I played over my head. At times I thought I was the good ship Lollipop to those caddies, which aggravated me to no end! In retrospect, I believe they just always negotiated a bet that benefited them more than it did me. However, they were good teachers, and honest.

By the time I was 16 I became what was considered a special caddy, which denoted that I was a caddy who knew how to play the game and to a certain extent, through my Monday experiences, knew how to bet the game. I could also "club" a player (advise which club to use), read a green, or possibly even give constructive hints on their golf swing, or how to play a shot. At times such advice could be dangerous or detrimental to your tip, depending upon who you were caddying for: besides possibly being the hero, you could also turn out to be the goat and be declared the reason for an errant or bad shot.

As every golfer knows, golfers have more excuses under the sun than there is sand in a sand trap! "I shouldn't have lost to you." "You shouldn't have won." "If I had only hit that shot." "If you hadn't sunk that putt." "If I hadn't hit that ball OB on eighteen."

Through those early golf experiences I did learn to play the game reasonably well, and I also learned to play a lot of the games that we still bet or wager on 25 years later.

To this day I still don't have a high level of proficiency, as evidenced by my 14 handicap. However, like most of us, and fortunately so, I don't play the game for a living, and therefore really enjoy the game and the action, and the competition that they generate. I hope the same proves true for you.

R.M.U.

The Players :

Skins Niblick · Shagbag · Mother Irons

Partner · The Kid · Angus McDivot

Dedicated to my parents, Bob and Eileen, for their continual support, encouragement and love.

"In golf, as in life, one is confronted with many up and down challenges, and those that address them, learn and eventually gain from those experiences."

R.M.U.

THE SIDE GAMES WE PLAY & WAGER

GAMES ONE

The games covered in this chapter are fairly simple, and though they can be played by themselves, they are usually played in conjunction with other games covered in later chapters.

The games involve different aspects of golf, from putting on the practice greens, maintaining tee honors, to three putting a green. Some of the games involve penalizing a player for hitting various types of errant shots, while on the other hand some of the games reward a player for hitting a good shot or for achieving a specific aspect of the game. Most of the games are applicable to any level of proficiency and all players can be involved. Therefore the following should provide you with the opportunity to introduce some friendly but fun competition to the round.

GARBARGE

This is a term that is used to describe other games that can be played while playing a standard 18-hole match like a Nassau or a best ball. In garbarge, a player or team can win points for achieving a par or a birdie in a variety of fashions, or possibly hitting a shot that is closest to the pin. Since the term garbarge means different things to different players, make sure that you know what the garbarge is that you are playing for. In some games of garbarge a player can lose more money than in the 18-hole Nassau or best ball game that is being played. The following are some of the types of garbarge .

BINGO-BANGO-BONGO (BINGLE BANGLE BUNGLE)

This is a game whereby the individual who is first on the green (BINGO) wins a point, or a quarter, or whatever the stakes. The same is true for the individual who is closest to the pin (BANGO) once everyone is on the green, and for the individual who first putts his ball into the cup (BONGO). Thus, first on, closest to the pin, and first in, decides who wins on each hole.

GREENIES—PLONKERS—BLUE PLATE SPECIAL—PROXIES

These are some of the terms used to describe the player whose shot is closest to the pin on par threes when hit in regulation. The player who achieves the greenie wins a point. However, a lot of golfers play that if the player getting the greenie does not at least par the hole then that greenie is lost. If a greenie is lost, or if no player gets a greenie because no one hit the green in regulation, most golfers play carryovers, so the next par three counts for two points. Also,

"There is no such individual as a born golfer." Ben Hogan

some golfers play that if one player gets all four greenies the points are doubled in value. When playing partners, such as in a Nassau, it is often common that a player achieving a greenie gets the greenie for the team so that each player on the team wins one point. Some also play that if the player getting the greenie putts for a birdie then the point value for that greenie is doubled. In the case of a carryover where the player getting the greenie also birdies the hole, then the point value is four times the original. In the event that no player gets a greenie after playing the par threes, many golfers play that the second shot to the last par three, that is closest to the pin, wins all four greenies or points.

CARPETS

In the course of playing greenies if a player or team wins every greenie then the payoff by the other player or team is doubled.

OUZLE—FOUZLE

In Scotland and England the player who hits a shot that is closest to the pin on par threes is said to have won an Ouzle from the other players. However, if the player who won the Ouzle three putts, then that player is now said to have the Fouzle, and instead of winning a unit or point from the other players, the player now pays the others. So an Ouzle is good and a Fouzle is bad!

EIGHTEEN—HOLE GREENIES

In California and some other areas they play greenies for all 18 holes so that the closest to the pin in the least amount of shots by any player in the foursome wins a greenie.

SANDIES—GRITTIES

This is a term used to describe a player who has hit into a greenside sand trap but still manages to par the hole. For each sandie a player gets, that player wins a point from the other players in the foursome.

SUPER SANDIE

A variation of a sandie in which a player achieves a par or better from a fairway bunker. If playing sandies then a super sandie is worth two points.

EXOTIC SANDIE

If playing sandies and a player achieves par or better after being in both a fairway and greenside bunker then that player is said to have achieved an exotic sandie and wins four points from each of the other players.

ARNIES or SEVIES

This is a term used to describe a player who, with the exception of par threes, on any hole is never on the fairway but still manages to par the hole. In such an event, that player wins a point from the other members of the foursome.

HOGANS

This is another side game in which a player wins a point from the other players by achieving a par or better on par fours and par fives and never has the ball out of the fairway. This side game does not include par threes, and greens must be reached in regulation. If you are also playing Arnies or Sevies, which have a point value of one, then Hogans should have a point value of two.

BARKIES or WOODIES

A term used to describe a player who hits any part of a tree, whether trunk, branch or limb; the player still achieves a par, and wins a point from the other players.

"Never bet with anyone you meet on the first tee, who has a deep suntan, a one iron in his bag and squinty eyes." Dave Marr

GARBARGE SKINS

Unless a player is tied or someone else shoots a lower score, a player wins a point for a par and two points for a birdie, and collects from each member of the group. (See a more detailed Skins explanation and format later in this chapter.)

FERRET or WATSON

A player who is off the green and chips into the hole, regardless of score achieved, wins a point from the other players.

GOLDEN FERRET

A player who is in a bunker and holes out, regardless of score achieved, wins two points from each of the other players.

MOLES

In this side game, a player who leaves a ball in a bunker after one shot, pays the others in the group one bet; if the player leaves the ball in the bunker on the second shot, then the player loses two bets to the others.

MURPHY

A player who is just off the green and is facing a chip shot can call a Murphy prior to chipping. Once a Murphy is called the player must then chip and one-putt to win a point from each of the other players. If the Murphy is not achieved, the player loses a point to the others.

"It's Old Man Par and you, match or medal. And Old Man Par is a patient soul, who never shoots a birdie and never incurs a buzzard. He's a patient old soul, Old Man Par. And if you would travel the long route with him, you must be patient too." Bobby Jones

DOUBLE MURPHY

In this case a player who has called a Murphy but has chipped off the green can now call a Double Murphy, which requires the player to chip and one-putt. If not succesful, the player loses another two points to each of the other players. If the player does chip and one-putt the player wins two points from the others. However, remember that the player lost a point when a Murphy was called, so the player on that hole would win a net one point from the others. If the player did not make the Double Murphy then that player loses three points on the hole to each of the others.

NICKLAUSES

This is a side bet in which the player in the group that has the longest drive in the fairway wins a point from the other players. This is a game played on all par fours and par fives.

SCRUFFY

In this situation a player who hits a really terrible tee shot calls a Scruffy and must then make a par or better on that hole. If a par or better is achieved then that player wins a point; if not, the player loses a point to the others. If a Scruffy is called all the others must agree that the tee shot was indeed terrible.

TITANIC

In this situation a player who hits a shot into the water but still achieves a par or better on the hole wins a point from the other players.

"If I died. . . it meant I couldn't play golf. No way was I giving up golf, so I gave up drinking." Bob Hope, L.A. Times '82

ANIMALS

In this game certain types of errant shots are designated as different types of animals. The player with the last animal during the round of play pays the other players whatever value has been placed on the animal. Usually each animal has the same value and in most games the value is one dollar. A shot hit out of bounds is a Gorilla, and a shot hit into the water is a Frog. On courses that don't have water or where water comes into play on only a few holes, any shot that hits a tree is a Tree Frog. A shot that is hit into any sand trap is a Camel, and anyone who has a three putt has a Snake. In this game the last player to have any animal or animals during the round pays the other players.

Additionally, if a player ends up with all four animals, that player then pays the others double. This game offers additional excitement because no one wants to end up having the Gorilla, Frog, Camel and the Snake!

POLEY

A Poley is a putting game played in the southeastern United States in which any player who sinks a putt that is longer than the length of the flagstick, on any hole, wins a point from the other players. If two or more players sink putts longer than the flagstick they each earn a point. At the end of the round add each player's points and the player with the most points wins an amount equal to the point differential between the other players, times the value of each point.

FLAGGY

This is another side bet in which a player or players win a point for hitting their tee shot on par threes within flagstick distance of the hole.

SKINS

This game is usually played by a threesome or foursome and the player who scores a par without being tied or beaten by another player wins a skin. If a player scores a birdie and no one else scores one, then that player gets two skins for that hole. In this game, two tie all tie. If a player scores an eagle, and no one else scores one, then the player gets three skins for that hole. In the case of a player scoring a birdie and the other players all scoring a par, the birdie shooter is the only one to get a skin for that hole. This can also be played so that the low score on a hole, providing there are no ties, gets a skin regardless of whether or not the low score is a par, or better.

In this game you can also play carryovers: if no one gets a skin on a particular hole, then on the next hole the player who gets a skin also gets a carryover skin from the previous hole. If four consecutive holes are tied, then the fifth hole will count for five skins if a player wins that hole without being tied.

At some clubs, when we have a large turnout of members, we play a pot skin game. Everyone who was in the skins game puts five dollars into the pot. After everyone has finished play, run down the scores on each hole, and the player who shot a birdie or a par with no other player beating that score or tying it gets one skin. After determining the total number of skins for the entire group, divide that number into the worth of the pot to determine the value of each skin. With 16 players for instance, where there are only five skins and one player has two of the five skins, then each skin is worth $16 and the player with two skins gets $32 out of the total pot of $80, with the balance going to the other three players with three skins.

With a large number of players with varying handicaps, we sometimes break the skin game up into two groups, one group playing just gross while the other plays with their handicaps. When a group is not too large, 12 to 16 players, and there isn't a huge discrepancy in handicaps, everyone will play a net skin game with full handicaps taken where they fall on the score card.

We have also played a skins game in which we have allowed only an arbitrary maximum handicap of 24 for each individual player; to determine skins we applied half of everyone's handicap to decide the skin winners.

In this game the maximum handicap allowed to determine skins is 12 and the handicap strokes are taken as they fall on the scorecard. Remember that two tie all tie in this game.

SEVEN UP

This is a putting game which is usually played on the practice putting green while you are waiting to tee off or possibly just practicing your putting with some friends. The game is played with at least two players, although I have played the game with as many as eight. This is a game with points earned or lost based upon the following: the player closest to the preselected hole after everyone has putted earns one point. If a player sinks a putt for a one-putt and no one else does so, the player earns two points. Anyone who three-putts on a hole loses three points, and the player who has the fewest putts on a hole without being tied earns a point. In this game two tie all tie with the exception of the players who three-putt. The first player to earn seven points wins the game and is paid by the other players based upon the difference in their point totals. If two players both earn seven points then everyone plays another hole, or more, until one player earns that eighth or ninth point with no other player having the same high point total. Whoever has honors

Regarding putts left short: *"The hole will not come to you, you must go to it!"* Bob Toski, Golf Digest 1990

in this game gets to select the next hole, which could conceivably be on the other side of the putting green, and each player must putt to it. Honors goes to the player who earns a point or points on the hole without being tied. The player who has the honors also putts first.

Also, in this game since we play with friends we mark our balls after putting if requested to; however, there are some players who don't allow marking of the ball at any time and, if you are stymied by another player's ball, that's just too bad. As with other games this can be played for ten cents per point, fifty cents per point or one dollar or more per point.

LOW PUTTS

This is another putting game that is played on the practice putting green. In this game, played by two to eight players, nine or possibly eighteen holes are played with each player putting to the selected hole and putting out. No "inside the leather" concessions, or gimmies in this game. Select an order of play so that each player gets to select a hole to putt to; the player who selects the hole putts first. The holes selected can require a short putt or a long putt across the practice green to a hole that is 40 to 50 feet away. The winner of this game is the player who has the fewest total putts for the holes that were played. In case of a tie the players can either split the winnings or can simply have a putt-off.

SEVEN ELEVEN

This is another putting game but involves just two players. This game is also played on the practice putting green, but each player uses two balls, and whoever has the honors putts the first ball and then the second ball to the selected hole, followed by the second player who putts both

"Nothing comes down slower than a golf handicap." Bobby Nichols, Never Say Never, '65

balls. In this game blocking your opponent is perfectly legal since you do not mark your balls. The closest ball to the hole earns a point regardless of whether or not the second ball is farthest from the hole. If, however, both of one player's balls are closer than the opponent's two balls, then that player earns two points. Also a one-putt earns a player three points.

However, if a player has a one-putt and the opponent has a one-putt on top of that, then the opponent earns six points and the player ends up with no points on that hole. If the player has two one-putts and the opponent has none, then the player earns six points. If the player has two one-putts and the opponent has one one-putt then the player earns three points. In the case of both players sinking both balls for one-putts then the second player would earn twelve points. In the case of the first player having only one one-putt while the opponent has two one-putts, the opponent would earn six points for topping the player's one-putt but would also earn another three points for the second one-putt resulting in nine points earned on that one hole.

In this game the first player to earn 11 points wins the game and is paid by the other player based upon the point differential between the two players. However, if a player earns seven points before the other player earns even a point, then the game is over because of the shutout and the bet is automatically doubled. Honors, or who putts first, goes to the player who earned points on the previous hole, and whoever has honors in this game does have an advantage over the other player. Remember that in this game blocking your opponent by lagging a putt to block the line of your opponent or blocking the hole to prevent your opponent from one-putting is legal. You don't mark your putts in this game.

SNAKE

This is a simple game in which the last player to three-putt a green during the round of play has to pay everyone

else a predetermined amount of money. If two players both three-putt the last green then the player that last putted for his three-putt has the snake and pays everyone else. Lagging for that two-putt is really important here, especially if someone else already has the snake!

SNAKES

This is the same type of game as Snake but in this game anyone who three-putts a green pays the other players in the foursome whatever amount has been decided before play. This type of game will either provide you with the monetary incentive to pay more attention to your putting and improve it or result in your developing the "yip" malady.

WALK WALK

This is a game that is played in the northwest (Washington and Oregon), in which any player can challenge another player who is about to putt that they will three-putt the green. If the player sinks the putt for a one-putt then the challenger loses the bet. If the player takes two putts to hole out then there is no winner—the bet is a push. If, however, the player three-putts the green then the player loses the bet. If you play this game so that you are playing for five dollars or ten dollars or even higher stakes, don't be surprised by players having their sphincter muscles really tighten up! Good players suddenly lose their putting touch and one learns what pressure is and realizes to a certain extent how a pro feels when faced with a three-foot putt to win top prize money.

TEE GAME

On the first tee you and your partner flip a coin or tee with your opponents to see who wins the honors to tee off first. The team that tees off first must hold the tee with their best ball; if they do they win one point apiece, if they lose the tee box honors they lose three points apiece. In this game a tie for best ball results in a push and the team that held the tee box still maintains honors on the next tee with no winning or losing of points. So, each team that has the tee box honors has the chance to either win a point or lose three points on each hole. The players I know who play this game usually play for either fifty cents or one dollar per point.

RABBIT

This game is played by three or more players and requires that the winner win four legs. Every player antes into the pot a prearranged amount and the winner takes all. In order to be the winner a player must win four holes outright from all the other players. A tie score does not count as a win. In this game carryovers do not count. Four individual holes must be won in order for a player to win the pot. The first player to win four holes without having another player tie or beat his score is the winner.

RABBITS

This is the same game as above, however, if a player does win four legs then another game of rabbit is automatically started with the same amount being played for. In the event that no player wins four legs after the completion of 18 holes and you are not going to play 27, then the player with the most legs wins the pot, unless decided otherwise prior to playing.

TICKS

This is a game played in Canada, and possibly elsewhere, in which players are awarded a point, or points, on each hole for accomplishing one or more of the following: one point for long drive in the fairway, one point for first on the green, one point for closest to the pin once all players are on the green, and one point for the first player to hole out.

"I play with friends, but we don't play friendly games."
Ben Hogan, Golf Digest '70

As might be noted, this game is somewhat similar to other point games, especially Bingo, Bango, Bongo. In this game, as in the other games, just add everyone's points at the end of the round. The winner is the player with the highest point total and is paid by the other players based upon the point differentials.

UMBRELLA

This is a team game of additional side bets. In this game a total of six points are up for grabs and are earned as follows: one point for closest to the pin in regulation, one point for low ball, one point for fewest combined putts, one point for a birdie and two points for low team score. There are no points won or lost in the case of ties. If a team wins all six points on a hole it is called an umbrella and in that event all points are doubled so that the losing team on the hole loses twelve points.

THE SIDE GAMES WE PLAY & WAGER

GAMES TWO

In this chapter some of the basic individual and team games are covered as well as some of the offshoots of those games. Games such as medal play, match play, and a Nassau are explained, as are some of the variations of those games.

These games usually involve the cumulative performance of a player for a round of golf rather than specific aspects of golf as covered in chapter one. Some of the games, with or without a partner, might only involve nine holes or six holes before partners might be changed or a new game is started. Additionally, with some of the games you will find that even though you didn't play in the same group with a player or players you can still arrange a bet or wager with that long-time rival or rivals!

MEDAL PLAY—STROKE PLAY

This is one of the basic forms of play in golf for both the professional and the amateur. It is simply the total number of strokes a player requires to complete a round of golf versus the opponent and their total strokes. Very simply the low score wins. You just play for a set amount of money for the 18 holes, whether it be $1.00 or $100.00. A variation holds that if there is a stroke differential between players that stroke differential is multiplied by an agreed-upon amount, with the high score player paying this amount to the low score player.

For instance, player A and player B are playing for five dollars per stroke differential. Player A shoots an 86 while player B shoots an 82. Based upon their bet, player A pays player B $20. If you have a foursome with the same level of playing ability, you can usually have individual games with the other players using the same format as above. Even though all four players might have the same handicap (which indicates their level of playing ability) within a shot or two of each other, I can just about guarantee that final scores of all players will show more than just a shot or two difference. Sometimes it just boils down to who's hot and who's not! (See scorecard example 2.0)

MEDAL PLAY HANDICAP

This is similar to medal play but handicaps are used to bring some parity to players who don't play at the same level of proficiency. In this game a player's handicap is subtracted from the gross score to result in a net score versus the net score of the other player. If you are playing partners then you can either play so that you are betting the low net best ball of the partners versus that of your opponents or the net total score of the partners versus that of your opponents. As in straight medal play you can bet a set amount of money for the low net score or have a bet based upon the stroke differential of the scores. In either case, when playing partners, both partners pay off the bet.

MATCH PLAY

This game is played hole by hole and the winner of the hole is the player having the lowest score. Each hole won counts as a plus while a hole lost counts as a minus. A hole that is tied is considered to be halved. The player at the end of the round of golf that has the most holes won after subtracting the holes lost is the winner. In this game your total gross score, which might be lower than your opponent's, does not necessarily mean you're going to win. I've shot an 82 and lost to a player who shot an 88. It just so happens that the player with the 88 had three bad holes (we are talking about triple bogey type bad holes), while the rest of the round was more than respectable. You bet this game the same way or ways that you do in medal play with or without a partner. (See scorecard example 2.1)

MATCH PLAY HANDICAP

This is the same game as straight match play with the exception that handicaps are used. There are a few ways to handle the handicap but the most common method involves the player having the lower handicap allowing the higher handicap player to deduct a stroke from the gross score achieved on the number of holes that are equal to the difference between their handicaps. As an example, if the difference between the handicaps is five then the high handicap player would take a stroke on the first five handicap stroke holes as indicated on the scorecard. Remember that the handicap stroke holes are not in order on the scorecard, but rather are indicated one through 18 based upon each hole's level of difficulty. You should also note that all the odd-numbered stroke holes are on the first nine holes and the even-numbered stroke holes are on the backside or second nine holes. So the handicap stroke hole that is indicated as

"Stroke play is a better test of golf, but match play is a better test of character." Joe Carr, Irish Amateur

MEDAL — STROKE PLAY

HOLE	1	2	3	4	5	6	7	8	9	Out
Black Tees	422	347	107	598	392	239	454	517	414	3490
Gold Tees	386	336	104	512	361	230	416	474	364	3183
Silver Tees	353	272	67	486	329	188	370	447	350	2862
PAR	4	4	3	5	4	3	4	5	4	36
Handicap	7	15	17	3	11	9	1	5	13	
PLAYER A (14)	5	5	3	5	6	5	5	5	5	44
PLAYER B (12)	5	4	3	6	5	3	4	5	4	39

INITIALS	10	11	12	13	14	15	16	17	18	In	Tot	Hcp	Net
	362	445	548	324	183	435	169	403	589	3458	6948		
	337	406	509	281	150	413	139	374	564	3173	6356		
	326	377	443	255	95	335	116	349	503	2799	5661		
	4	4	5	4	3	4	3	4	5	36	72		
	16	6	4	12	14	2	18	8	10				
A	5	4	5	6	3	5	4	4	6	42	86		
B	5	5	7	3	3	4	4	6	6	43	82		

Scorecard 2.0

In the above Straight Medal or Stroke Play game Player B wins by 4 shots.

one is supposed to be the most difficult hole to play on the course. The stroke holes are intended to be an equalizer between players of differing handicaps, but, be cautious of the sandbagger with an inflated handicap!

Another way in which the game can be played is to have both players take their full handicaps wherever they fall on the scorecard, with the low score, regardless of whether it is a gross or a net score, winning that hole. In this game, as in others, you can bet a set amount for whoever wins the most holes or you can wager a set amount multiplied by the number of holes the winner wins by. This game can be and often is played with partners; the format and the betting are the same as if playing a singles match. Remember that if you are playing partners, both players pay off to the winning players whatever the prearranged bet was.

NASSAU

This is probably the game that golfers are most familiar with and that is most commonly played. The game is basically three matches with the front nine holes comprising one match, the back nine holes another, and the 18 hole total making the third match. So, if a player is going to play a two dollar Nassau, it means that the front side is being played for two dollars, the backside for two dollars, and the total is worth two dollars.

In a Nassau bet each hole is played as an individual match so that a player who scores a par four to beat an opponent who shot a five goes one up. On the next hole, if the player who shot a par four on the first hole scores a bogey five on the second hole but still beats the opponent who shot a double bogey, player then goes two up. If both players on the third hole shoot bogeys, there is no blood and the player who shot the par four on the first hole still remains two up, or plus two. The match is played in this manner for the first nine holes and whoever is up, or is plus one, or plus two, or plus three, wins the front side.

The back nine holes are played the same way but the players start a new match on the tenth hole. Whoever wins the tenth hole goes one up or plus one. Once again, whoever is up after playing the back nine wins that side. If both players come out even then that side is a push and no one wins. However, let's say that the player who shot that par four on the first hole wins the front side by plus three and that the player lost the back side to the opponent by minus two, then the player would win the total by plus one. In the event that our players each win a side by plus three, then they played all day for a tie. No one wins.

This game can become more interesting with the introduction of presses. A press is when a player who is losing wants to start another bet possibly to offset the one they are losing, or possibly to bring the first bet to even and win the press bet to win that side. A press bet is just another bet, like the one in progress, but it starts at whichever hole the player requests. In most cases, a press bet is initiated once a player is two down. As an example, let's say that our press player is two down after two holes and on the third tee presses his opponent. Our player then wins the third hole and as a result his bet status is one down on the original bet and one up on the press bet. Let's say that our press player then wins the fourth hole and therefore goes to even on the original bet and two up on his press bet. However, now his opponent is down two on the press bet and therefore decides to press the press bet, which is perfectly legal. So with this new scenario, let's say that our press player loses the fifth hole after winning two holes, and as a result goes to minus one on the original bet, one up on his press bet, and now one down on his

"We're not trying to humiliate the greatest players in the world. We're trying to identify them." Frank Tatum, regarding the tough conditions of the U.S. Open courses, Sports Illustrated '84

MATCH AND NASSAU GAMES

As indicated below Player A gets 2 shots from Player B due to handicap differential (shot holes circled). Scoring is from Player A's standpoint.

HOLE	1	2	3	4	5	6	7	8	9	Out
Black Tees	422	347	107	598	392	239	454	517	414	3490
Gold Tees	386	336	104	512	361	230	416	474	364	3183
Silver Tees	353	272	67	486	329	188	370	447	350	2862
PAR	4	4	3	5	4	3	4	5	4	36
Handicap	7	15	17	3	11	9	1	5	13	
PLAYER A (14)	5	5	3	5	6	5	⑤	5	5	44
PLAYER B (12)	5	4	3	6	5	3	4	5	4	39
MATCH	-	-1	-1	-	-1	-2	-2	-2	-3	
NASSAU	-	-1	-1	-	-1	-2	-2	-2	-3	-3

INITIALS	10	11	12	13	14	15	16	17	18	In	Tot	Hcp	Net
	362	445	548	324	183	435	169	403	589	3458	6948		
	337	406	509	281	150	413	139	374	564	3173	6356		
	326	377	443	255	95	335	116	349	503	2799	5661		
	4	4	5	4	3	4	3	4	5	36	72		
	16	6	4	12	14	2	18	8	10				
A	5	4	5	6	3	(5)	4	4	6	42	86		
B	5	5	7	3	3	4	4	6	6	43	82		
	-3	-2	-1	-2	-2	-2	-2	-1	-1		-1		
	-	+1	+2	+1	+1	+1	+1	+2	+2	+2	-1		

In the match game Player A loses by 1 hole to Player B. In the Nassau Game Player A loses the front side −3, but wins the back side +2. Player A therefore loses the total Nassau −1 and loses one bet.

opponent's press bet. Let's say that the nine holes end with our press player losing the original bet down two, wins his press bet plus one but loses on his opponent's press bet two down. Our press player would therefore lose one bet since his press bet negated one of his opponent's bets.

In this game it doesn't matter if one of the bets is won by four or five up; it can still be negated and result in a push even if another bet is only won by one up. In a Nassau bet you can have as many presses as are accepted, however, only the original bet will count to the total after you have played 18 holes.

Additionally, this is a game that can be played not only by two players but also by a threesome, and in more cases than not by foursomes. In the case of a threesome each player can have an individual Nassau game with the other two players. In the case of a foursome the players can either play individual matches among themselves or play both a team match coupled with individual matches. The team matches and their various formats are described next in this chapter. (See scorecard example 2.1)

PRESS or ROLL THE DRUMS

This is a bet made during a match in addition to the original bet and is made by the player or team that is losing. The press bet, which in the majority of cases involves a Nassau match or a variation of the Nassau, runs only for the holes remaining to be played on either the front nine holes or the back nine holes at the point that the press bet was declared. In most cases a press bet is usually called when a player or team is at least two down. The player or team that is ahead does not have to accept the press; however, it is customary and more of a tradition to accept the press. Though local rules vary, press bets have been called when anyone is angry, meaning press at anytime, or a press bet must be called on the hole where a player or team goes two down. Other local rules call for automatic press bets when a player or team goes two down on any bet, whether it is the original bet or a subsequent press bet.

NASSAU—PARTNERS

This game is played with the same format as above but with a partner. I've played this game several ways, one of which is just best ball of the partners versus that of your opponent's. Another way to play is with each hole being worth two points, one point for low ball and one point for low total. If there is a tie for low ball between the teams the hole is halved for the low ball point. If there is also a tie for low total between the teams then this point is also halved and no points are won or lost. This is a good game because it keeps everyone in the match. As an example, you shoot a triple bogey seven while your partner gets a birdie three while your opponents both shoot bogey fives. In this case you and your partner would win one point for low ball and push with your opponents for low total since you both had tens. Press bets are played the same way you would in an individual Nassau match. (See scorecard example 2.2)

NASSAU—PARTNERS LOW BALL, LOW TOTAL

This is another variation of the Nassau that you play with a partner. In this game low ball is played as an individual match between the teams and so is the low total. Going back to the example above where you shot the triple bogey seven and your partner shot the birdie three and your opponents both shot fives, in this game, it would result in your team being plus one on the low ball match and even on the low

"Watching Sam Snead practice hitting golf balls is like watching a fish practice swimming." John Schlee, Golf Digest '77

34

total match. If on the next hole you and your partner shoot par fours while your opponents again shoot bogey fives, you win both the low ball and the low total. You would now be plus two on the low ball match and plus one on the low total match. Press bets are handled the same as in a straight Nassau game. In the above example, the team that was down two on the low ball match could press, if they desired. (See scorecard example 2.3)

NASSAU—PARTNERS LOW BALL, HIGH BALL

This is just another variation on the above but, in this case, the team that has the individual high ball loses a point. As in the example above where you shot the seven and your partner shot the three while your opponents both shot fives, in this game you win a point for the low ball and lose a point for having the high score with a seven. If you are playing two points a hole and not having separate team matches for low ball or high ball, then your match would be even. If, on the other hand, you are having separate matches then your team would be plus one on the low ball and minus one for the high ball. Press bets are handled the same way as in the previous Nassau examples. (See scorecard example 2.3)

NASSAU FOUR WAYS

The format for this game is the same as for a normal Nassau bet with the exception that the back side counts for two bets. As an example, if you or your team is playing a two-dollar Nassau the front side will count two dollars, the back side will count four dollars, and the total 18 will count two dollars. Therefore you or your team can conceivably win a total of eight dollars for the match.

"The only shots you can be dead sure of are those you've had already." Byron Nelson

NASSAU GAMES

Low Ball/Low Total & Low Ball/High Ball with player A with a 12 handicap, player B with a 14 handicap, versus Player C with an 11 handicap, player D with a 15 handicap. Teams will play even since total handicaps of both teams equal 26. Scoring is from player AB's standpoint.

HOLE	1	2	3	4	5	6	7	8	9	Out
Black Tees	422	347	107	598	392	239	454	517	414	3490
Gold Tees	386	336	104	512	361	230	416	474	364	3183
Silver Tees	353	272	67	486	329	188	370	447	350	2862
PAR	4	4	3	5	4	3	4	5	4	36
Handicap	7	15	17	3	11	9	1	5	13	
PLAYER A (12)	5	4	3	6	5	3	4	5	4	39
PLAYER B (14)	5	5	3	5	6	5	5	5	5	44
PLAYER C (11)	4	4	3	6	4	3	5	5	5	39
PLAYER D (15)	6	5	4	7	6	4	5	6	4	47
LOW BALL/LOW TOT.	-1	-1	0	+2	0	-1	+1	+2	+2	+2
LOW BALL/HIGH BALL	-	-	+1	+3	+2	+1	+2	+3	+3	+3

INITIALS	10	11	12	13	14	15	16	17	18	In	Tot	Hcp	Net
	362	445	548	324	183	435	169	403	589	3458	6948		
	337	406	509	281	150	413	139	374	564	3173	6356		
	326	377	443	255	95	335	116	349	503	2799	5661		
	4	4	5	4	3	4	3	4	5	36	72		
	16	6	4	12	14	2	18	8	10				
A	5	5	7	3	3	4	4	6	6	43	82		
B	5	4	5	6	3	5	4	4	6	42	86		
C	4	5	6	5	3	4	4	3	6	40	79		
D	5	5	6	5	3	5	5	6	5	45	92		
	-2	-	+1	+3	+3	+3	+4	+2	-	-	+2		
	-1	-	-	-	-	-	+1	-	-1	-1	+2		

Scorecard 2.2

In the above example team AB in the Low Ball/Low Total match win the front side, tie the back side and win the total match +2. Team AB therefore wins two bets. In the above Low Ball/High Ball match, team AB wins the front side +3 but loses the back side −1, therefore they win the total match +2. Therefore team AB wins one bet.

NASSAU GAME

The Low Ball/Low Total and the Low Ball/High Ball matches are played as a separate Nassau game with automatic presses when 2 down as illustrated below. The teams are Players AB versus Players CD with the scoring from Team AB's standpoint.

HOLE	1	2	3	4	5	6	7	8	9	Out
Black Tees	422	347	107	598	392	239	454	517	414	3490
Gold Tees	386	336	104	512	361	230	416	474	364	3183
Silver Tees	353	272	67	486	329	188	370	447	350	2862
PAR	4	4	3	5	4	3	4	5	4	36
Handicap	7	15	17	3	11	9	1	5	13	
PLAYER A (12)	5	4	3	6	5	3	4	5	4	39
B (14)	5	5	3	5	6	5	5	5	5	44
PLAYER C (11)	4	4	3	6	4	3	5	5	5	39
D (15)	6	5	4	7	6	4	5	6	4	47
LOW BALL	-1	-1	-1	-	-1	-1	-	-	-	-
LOW TOTAL	-	-	+1	+2	+1 / -1	- / -2	+1 / -1	+2	+2	+2
LOW BALL	-1	-1	-1	-	-1	-1	-	-	-	-
HIGH BALL	+1	+1	+2	+3 / +1	+3 / +1	+2 / -	+2 / -	+3 / +1	+3 / +1	+3 / +1

In the above example Players AB break even in the Low Ball but lose the press bet, so they lose one bet. In regard to the Low Total game Players AB win the front +2, tie the back, win the overall +2 but lose one press bet. Therefore team AB wins one bet. Overall in the Low Ball/Low Total games the teams would break even.

INITIALS	10	11	12	13	14	15	16	17	18	In	Tot	Hcp	Net
	362	445	548	324	183	435	169	403	589	3458	6948		
	337	406	509	281	150	413	139	374	564	3173	6356		
	326	377	443	255	95	335	116	349	503	2799	5661		
	4	4	5	4	3	4	3	4	5	36	72		
	16	6	4	12	14	2	18	8	10				
A	5	5	7	3	3	4	4	6	6	43	82		
B	5	4	5	6	3	5	4	4	6	42	86		
C	4	5	6	5	3	4	4	3	6	40	79		
D	5	5	6	5	3	5	5	6	5	45	92		
LB	-1	-	+1	+2	+2/-	+2/-	+2/-	+1/-1	-/-2	-/-2	-		
LT	-1	-	-	+1	+1	+1	+2	+1/-1	-/-2	-/-2	+2		
LB	-1	-	+1	+2	+2/-	+2/-	+2/-	+1/-1	-/-2	-/-2	-		
HB	-	-	-1	-2	-2/-	-2/-	-1/+1	-1/+1	-1/+1	-1/+1	+2		

Scorecard 2.3

Players AB in the High Ball game win the front +3, and a press +1, lose the back side −1 but win the total +2 and win a press bet. Therefore Players AB in the High Ball game would win three bets. Overall in the Low Ball/High Ball games team AB would win a total of two bets.

NASSAU SIX WAYS

In this variation on the Nassau bet, the front side counts as one bet, the back side counts as two bets, and the total for the 18 counts as three bets. The reasoning for this type of Nassau is that if a player or team beats the opponents on the front side by three or four up but lose the back side by one or two they should at least win something which would not be the case in a Nassau-Four Way. In the case of a two dollar match a player or team can conceivably win twelve dollars for the match.

ROBBINS or SIXES or SIX HOLE SWITCH

These are all names that Texans use to describe a foursome in which you change partners after every six holes. This allows you to play with everyone as a partner. Partners are usually decided by a ball toss or by one player flipping a tee and the partner being chosen by whoever the tip of the tee is pointing to. I've played this game several ways: a straight best ball of the partners, low ball—low total, or total score of the partners. You can bet on the winner of the six hole match or bet a set amount times the point or score differential between the teams. Usually Robbins is played while other individual games are being played.

ROBBINS NASSAU

This is played the same as a Robbins game, however, you break up each six-hole match into a Nassau bet with the first three holes being the front side and the last three holes being the back side, and then figuring the total for the six holes. This is done for each six-hole match that you play with a different partner. This game is bet the same as you would a regular 18 hole Nassau match and can be played as a best ball, low ball—low total, or total score of the partners.

"Golf is a good walk spoiled." Mark Twain

STABLEFORD

This is a game in which you play against everyone else. It is based on a point system in which a player wins or loses points as determined by score. The points are determined as follows: eight points for a double eagle, five for an eagle, two for a birdie, zero for a par, minus one for a bogey and minus three for double bogey or worse. Since the majority of golfers are not professionals, this game is usually played with golfers using their full handicaps to arrive at a net score from which they determine their point awards, either positive or negative. The value of a point is whatever everyone agrees to, whether ten cents or one dollar per point. The winner is the player who, at the end of 18 holes, has more points than any other player. The other players pay the winner the difference in their point totals from the winner's point total, times the value of each point. You can also play that third place pays off second place and that fourth place pays off both second and third place. If you decide to play the latter, fourth place could prove to be expensive since you pay everyone! Have them pay for drinks! (See scorecard example 2.4)

BRITISH STABLEFORD

Another Stableford game played primarily in Britain, this one awards points to players based upon the following: one point for a bogey, two points for a par, three points for a birdie and four points for an eagle. This game can be played with full handicaps, and the player who earns the highest number of points wins.

JOKER STABLEFORD

This game is played in Spain and uses the same format as the Stableford previously explained with the one exception that each player is allowed, prior to teeing off, one hole on the front side and one hole on the back side as a joker hole. The player who declares a hole a joker hole gets whatever points were earned for that hole doubled. If two or more players use the same hole as a joker hole, then the points earned by each individual player who declared the hole a joker hole are doubled. The player with the most points at the end of the round is the winner, and is paid by the other players based upon the point differentials.

EAST COAST POINT GAME

This is another point game played primarily on the east coast of the United States, and can be played by two, three or four players, and conceivably more. In this game, played with full handicaps, players can earn points on each hole based upon the following format: five points for an eagle, three points for a birdie, two points for a par and one point for a bogey. Each player on each hole is in essence playing against himself. As in some other games described in this and other chapters, a player is not concerned about playing in comparison to the other players but rather how they play in comparison to par. The winner in this game is the player who has achieved the highest point total for the 18 holes. The winner is then paid by the other players based upon point differentials. Point value is whatever has been decided prior to playing the round.

CHAIRMAN

This is another threesome game, in which the first player to win a hole regardless of score, using full handicaps, and without being tied, becomes the chairman, and assumes the chair. If the chairman wins the next hole then the chairman wins a point from the two other players. If the chairman is tied on a hole, there are no points lost or won and the chairman retains the chair. If one of the other two players wins a hole then that player becomes the chairman, but there are no points lost or won. Therefore, it becomes obvious that in order to win points, a player has to win two holes, possibly separated by holes that might have been tied, before money is won or lost. (See scorecard example 2.5)

"The mind messes up more shots than the body." Tommy Bolt

STABLEFORD

A game with players getting full handicaps (handicaps holes are circled) with points earned or lost on each hole as indicated below each player's score.

HOLE	1	2	3	4	5	6	7	8	9	Out
Black Tees	422	347	107	598	392	239	454	517	414	3490
Gold Tees	386	336	104	512	361	230	416	474	364	3183
Silver Tees	353	272	67	486	329	188	370	447	350	2862
PAR	4	4	3	5	4	3	4	5	4	36
Handicap	7	15	17	3	11	9	1	5	13	
PLAYER A (12)	⑤	4	3	⑥	⑤	③	④	⑤	4	39
	0	0	0	0	0	2	2	2	0	6 PTS.
B (14)	⑤	5	3	⑤	⑥	⑤	⑤	⑤	⑤	44
	0	-1	0	2	-1	-1	0	2	0	1 PT.
C (11)	④	4	3	⑥	④	③	⑤	⑤	5	39
	2	0	0	0	2	2	0	2	-1	7 PTS.
D (15)	⑥	⑤	4	⑦	⑥	④	⑤	⑥	④	47
	-1	0	-1	-1	-1	0	0	0	2	-2 PTS.

INITIALS	10	11	12	13	14	15	16	17	18	In	Tot	Hcp	Net
	362	445	548	324	183	435	169	403	589	3458	6948		
	337	406	509	281	150	413	139	374	564	3173	6356		
	326	377	443	255	95	335	116	349	503	2799	5661		
	4	4	5	4	3	4	3	4	5	36	72		
	16	6	4	12	14	2	18	8	10				
A	5	(5)	(7)	(3)	3	(4)	4	(6)	(6)	43	82		
	-1	0	-1	5	0	2	-1	-1	0	3 PTS	9 PTS. TOTAL		
B	5	(4)	(5)	(6)	(3)	(5)	4	(4)	(6)	42	86		
	-1	2	2	-1	2	0	-1	2	0	5 PTS	6 PTS. TOTAL		
C	4	(5)	(6)	5	3	(4)	4	(3)	(6)	40	79		
	0	0	0	-1	0	2	-1	5	0	5 PTS	12 PTS. TOTAL		
D	5	(5)	(6)	(5)	(3)	(5)	5	(6)	(5)	45	92		
	-1	0	0	0	2	0	-3	-1	2	-1 PT.	-3 PTS. TOTAL		

Scorecard 2.4

In this particular game Player C would win 3 points from Player A, 6 points from Player B and 15 points from Player D. If you were to play a team Stableford with AB versus CD then team AB would win from team CD 6 points (15 points total for team AB minus 9 points total for team CD).

PARROT

This is the same game as Chairman, however, instead of being in the chair if a player wins a hole outright, the player is said to be the parrot and is now "on the perch." The same format as Chairman is used to earn points.

COYOTE KILL

This is a game that is suited for golfers who belong to a club or a group of golfers who get together every week or every other week and who play with a group of eight or more. With this game each player antes a set amount into a common pot, whether one dollar or twenty dollars per player. The game to be played is determined by the previous winners after everyone has paid their antes. The games usually played are: low gross, low net (100% handicap), skins game (50% handicap), Stableford (100% handicap). This game usually has at least 16 players, who use a deck of cards to determine partners. The two players who pull the same color ace, king, queen or jack become partners, e.g., the two black aces are one team, the two red aces are another team. Regardless of the game that is played, this type of game involves having different players as partners and being involved in a variety of games.

HOGAN POINT GAME

This is played by a twosome, threesome or foursome with everyone playing by themselves or playing this game in addition to any other game you arrange, such as a Nassau. This game simply awards one point to each player who hits the fairway on the drive, hits the green in regulation, or one or two putts, and two points for scoring a birdie. Point differences after 18 holes decide how much each player pays to the player with the highest point total. In some cases the low total player and the second low total player pay off all other players.

47

CHAIRMAN

In the game below players are playing with full handicaps (handicaps are in parentheses), with the shots due each player indicated by dots on the appropriate shot holes. A player who becomes Chairman is indicated by a circle.

HOLE	1	2	3	4	5	6	7	8	9	Out
Black Tees	422	347	107	598	392	239	454	517	414	3490
Gold Tees	386	336	104	512	361	230	416	474	364	3183
Silver Tees	353	272	67	486	329	188	370	447	350	2862
PAR	4	4	3	5	4	3	4	5	4	36
Handicap	7	15	17	3	11	9	1	5	13	
PLAYER A (15)	④	5	3	7	5	4	6	6	⑤	45
B (18)	5	6	4	6	5	5	5	7	6	49
C (23)	5	6	5	⑦	6	4	⑤	5	6	49

INITIALS	10	11	12	13	14	15	16	17	18	In	Tot	Hcp	Net
	362	445	548	324	183	435	169	403	589	3458	6948		
	337	406	509	281	150	413	139	374	564	3173	6356		
	326	377	443	255	95	335	116	349	503	2799	5661		
	4	4	5	4	3	4	3	4	5	36	72		
	16	6	4	12	14	2	18	8	10				
A	4	5	5	4	5	6	4	(4)	6	43	88		
B	5	5	8	4	(3)	6	4	6	6	47	96		
C	6	5	6	4	4	(5)	3	6	6	45	94		

Scorecard 2.5

As indicated above Player A becomes the Chairman on hole 1 and wins 1 point. Player C becomes Chairman on hole 4 but wins no points. Player C assumes the chair on hole 7 and wins 1 point before losing the chair to Player A, on hole 9. Player A retains the chair until hole 14 but wins no points. On hole 14 Player B assumes the chair but immediatley loses such to Player C on hole 15. Player C as Chairman wins 1 point but loses the chair to Player A on hole 17. Player A wins no points since all players tie on hole 18. As a result, Player A wins no points for the game, Player B loses 3 points and Player C wins 3 points.

AUSTRALIAN HOGAN

This is a point game for the more advanced player in which points are earned or lost based upon the following format: one point for hitting the fairway on your drive or a point lost for not hitting the fairway, a point for hitting the green in regulation or a point lost for not hitting the green in regulation, two points for a par, three points for a birdie and four points for an eagle or better, while on the other hand a point is lost for a bogey, two points lost for a double bogey and three points lost for anything over a double bogey. Once again, total points after 18 holes decides who pays whom.

POINT GAME

This is a game very similar to Hogan, but points are awarded on the following basis: one for a proxy (ball closest to the hole), two points for a birdie, one point for the high ball and one point for the low ball. The total possible points for a hole is five. If there is a tie for low or high ball no points are given. In this game even if a player is having a really bad hole, they can still win a point. Even with a score approaching double digits, the player can still possibly get two points for the hole, by not only having the high score but also by getting the proxy. Total points after 18 holes determines who pays whom, once again based upon the point differentials of the players.

SEVEN POINT GAME

The following is played with one twosome playing against another twosome with the possibility of 7 points being won on every hole. The points that can be won are as follows: two points for the twosome with the low ball of the foursome, two points for the twosome that does not have the high ball of the foursome, one point for a proxy in regulation, one point for a birdie, and one point for the twosome with the least amount of total putts. In case of a tie no points are won.

This game can be played using gross scores, providing that

there is not a large discrepancy in handicaps between the twosomes. However, in most cases this game is played with full handicaps so that net scores are used in determining the points won on each hole.

This game also allows one press bet per nine holes, and this press bet is called a "knee bend." The "knee bend" however, can only be called by the twosome that is down in points and is only applicable for hole number 9 and number 18. Also if the "knee bend" is to be called it must be called on the 8th hole for the press on the 9th, or on the 17th for the press on 18. If the "knee bend" is called then all points are doubled in value for just the 9th hole, and/or the 18th hole. The winner is the twosome with the most points at the end of the round. Winnings are paid by each player of the losing twosome in an amount equal to the difference in point totals times the value of each point.

POINT A HOLE
This is a bet in which you play each hole for a predetermined point value and you play each hole as an individual match. At the end of 18 holes whoever has the most points wins, and winnings are determined by subtracting the point total from the other individual point totals multiplied by the value of the point.

LOW NET FOURSOME
If you have a good outing with three or four foursomes or more this can be played in conjunction with other matches or bets. Everyone antes into a common pot and the winning foursome splits the pot. The game involves the total score of each foursome less the handicaps of each player in the foursome. The low net score wins the pot.

"I never played a round when I didn't learn something new about the game." Ben Hogan

PER YARD PER HOLE or YARDAGES

I haven't heard of this game being played too often, but I imagine it could turn out to be quite expensive for a player or a team not playing very well if they are playing for high stakes. Very simply, it is a game in which you are betting on every hole and the bet on every hole is predetermined by the yardage length of the hole. As an example, if the first hole is a par four of 400 yards, then the winner of the first hole wins 400 times whatever you are playing for. If you are playing for one dollar per yard, then the player or team who wins the first hole wins $400. If the average length of a golf course is approximately 6,000 yards, this type of game can prove to be expensive.

BLIND DRAW BEST BALL

This is a game played with eight or more players. Everyone places into the pot a set amount of money, whether fifty cents or five dollars, and then everyone goes out and plays their regular game. After everyone has finished play, everyone's name is placed in a hat and twosomes are drawn out of the hat to form the blind draw twosomes. The twosome's best ball net score (full handicap strokes taken where indicated on the scorecard) on each hole is determined for the 18 holes and the winner is the twosome with the lowest score. With twelve or more players we usually pay three places.

BOGEY

Lee Trevino supposedly played this game prior to playing on the professional tour. It is usually played by golfers with a high level of proficiency, or with low handicaps. The first player in the foursome to shoot a bogey or worse without

"You don't know what pressure is until you play for five bucks with only two in your pocket." Lee Trevino, Newsweek '71

BOGEY GAME

In the scorecard example below the players are playing gross score. The bogey players who pay are circled and the players who score a subsequent bogey are underlined. In the example below four bogey games are played through 18 holes.

HOLE	1	2	3	4	5	6	7	8	9	Out
Black Tees	422	347	107	598	392	239	454	517	414	3490
Gold Tees	386	336	104	512	361	230	416	474	364	3183
Silver Tees	353	272	67	486	329	188	370	447	350	2862
PAR	4	4	3	5	4	3	4	5	4	36
Handicap	7	15	17	3	11	9	1	5	13	
PLAYER A (6)	4	4	2	6	4	3	5	⑥	4	38
B (4)	4	3	3	5̲	4	3	5̲	5	5	37
C (5)	⑤	4	3	6	4	3	6	5	4	40
D (7)	4	4	3	5	5̲	3	4	5	6	39

In the above example Player C becomes the first Bogey player (hole 1) and therefore loses 3 points to Player A (bogey on hole 4), loses 6 points to Player B (bogey on hole 7), loses 4 points to Player D (bogey on hole 5). Player A becomes the next Bogey player (hole 8) and loses 1 point to Player B (bogey on hole 9), loses 3 points to Player C (bogey on hole 11), loses 1 point to Player D (bogey on hole 9). The next Bogey players are Players B and D (hole 12), who both lose 3 points to Player A (bogey on hole 15), and lose 3 points to Player C (bogey on hole 15). The next Bogey player is Player B

INITIALS	10	11	12	13	14	15	16	17	18	In	Tot	Hcp	Net
	362	445	548	324	183	435	169	403	589	3458	6948		
	337	406	509	281	150	413	139	374	564	3173	6356		
	326	377	443	255	95	335	116	349	503	2799	5661		
	4	4	5	4	3	4	3	4	5	36	72		
	16	6	4	12	14	2	18	8	10				
	5	5	5	4	3	6	3	5	5	41	79		
	4	4	(6)	3	3	5	(4)	4	5	38	75		
	4	5	5	4	2	6	3	5	5	39	79		
	4	4	(6)	5	3	4	3	4	5	38	77		

Scorecard 2.6

(hole 16) and loses 1 point to Player A (bogey on hole
17), loses 1 point to Player C (bogey on hole 17), and
loses 3 points to Player D.

Results of the above Bogey game are as follows:

Player A	+3−5+6+1	= 5 total points won
Player B	+6+1−6−5	= 4 total points lost
Player C	−13+3+6+1	= 3 total points lost
Player D	+4+1−6+3	= 2 total points won

another player scoring a bogey or worse on the hole pays a set amount to the other players. Play continues until each individual player shoots a bogey or worse. So, if player A scores a bogey on the first hole and all other players par the hole, then A pays. If player B in the foursome shoots a bogey on the second hole, then B only gets paid by A for the first hole. If player C bogeys the sixth hole, then C would be paid five times the agreed amount. If player D shoots a par round of golf, then player D receives from player A 18 times the agreed amount. If everyone gets a bogey or worse prior to the finish of 18 holes, after the last player has been paid, the foursome starts another game which is played the same way.

This game also works with players utilizing their full handicaps and taking their shots where they fall on the scorecard. Once again, the player who first scores a bogey or worse, whether it be a gross or net bogey without another player scoring a bogey or worse, pays each of the players the agreed upon amount on each hole played until each player finally scores a bogey or worse. (See scorecard example 2.6)

DOUBLE BOGEY or "DB'S"

This game is an offshoot of the Bogey game and is probably more suited for players who do not have low handicaps. In this game, with or without handicaps, the player who first shoots a double bogey or worse without another player doing so pays the other players an agreed upon amount on each hole that is played until each of the players scores a double bogey or worse. Once all players have scored a double bogey or worse, another game can be started for the balance of the holes to be played. Remember that in this game the player who first shoots the double bogey pays each player on each hole played until the player shoots a bogey or worse. Another game is not started until the last player in the foursome has shot that double bogey. This is a game that can be played for ten cents a hole or ten dollars a hole.

TRIVIA
MAKING THE TURN !!

The first "OPEN (BRITISH) CHAMPIONSHIP" was held in 1860 at the Prestwick Club in Scotland and had eight participants.

The first United States OPEN CHAMPIONSHIP was held in 1895.

United States golf got started in 1888, in Yonkers, N.Y.

The most expensive country club in the world is in Japan. Membership at the Koganei Country Club, Tokyo, costs $2,344,000.

Golf bags were initiated around 1895, prior to which players or caddies carried clubs and equipment by hand.

Every hole at the Manila Golf and Country Club was named after a different species of tree on the course: Narra, Acacia, Chico, Dao, Pili, Caballero, Santol, Banana, Avocado, Guava, Launa, Kakawate, Nanka, Ipil, Tamarind, Agoho, Dapdap, Mango.

The first hole-in-one ever recorded was by Tom Morris, Jr. in the 1868 Open Championship, on the eighth hole at Prestwick.

Schlaff—meaning that the ball has been mis-hit because the clubhead has hit the ground first—is one of the oldest terms in golf and is probably of ancient Scottish origin. In the States we say that the shot was hit "fat." Maybe "schlaff" is more appropriate just by the sound of the word!

Longest hole-in-one on a straightway by a man: 447 yards by Robert Mitera, of Omaha, on the 10th hole at the Miracle Hills Golf Club, Omaha, Nebraska.

Longest hole-in-one on a straightway by a woman: 393 yards by Marie Robie, Wollaston, Massachusetts, on the first hole at Furnace Brook Golf Club, Wollaston, Massachusetts, in 1949.

Most holes in one round: 3 by Dr. Joseph Boydstone, Bakersfield, California, on the third, fourth, and ninth holes at the Bakersfield Country Club on October 10, 1962.

Longest double eagle by a man: 647 yards, by Chief Petty Officer Kevin Murray on the second hole at the Guam Navy Golf Club in 1982.

Longest double eagle by a woman: 509 yards, by Mrs. William Jenkins, Sr., Baltimore, Maryland, on the twelfth hole at Longview Golf Club in Cockeysville, Maryland, 1965.

Electric golf carts were first used for golf at the Thunderbird Golf Club, United States, 1949.

Golf clubhead covers were first sold at St. Andrews, Scotland in 1916. They were designed by a Japanese student, Seilchi Takahata, while in England.

The "YIPS" was a term that was first coined by professional, Tommy Armour in the 1930s to describe the nervous twitch that afflicts many golfers when putting.

58

The most consecutive birdies in one round was ten and was achieved by professional John Irwin at the St. Catharine's Golf and Country Club, Ontario, Canada, in 1984.

Worlds longest course is the par 77, 8,325 yard International Golf Club, Bolton, Massachusetts.

Longest Par 3 — 270 yards, sixteenth, International Golf Club, Bolton, Massachusetts.

Longest Par 4 — 500 yards, sixth, Eisenhower Golf Club, City of Industry, California.

Longest Par 5 — 710 yards, seventeenth, Palmira Golf and Country Club, St. Johns, Indiana.

Longest Par 6 — 747 yards, seventeenth, Black Mountain Golf Course, North Carolina.

Longest Par 7 — 948 yards, sixth, Koolan Island Golf Club, Western Australia.

Largest Tournament—The Volkswagen Grand Prix Open Amateur Championship (UK) attracted a record 321,778 competitors (206,820 men, and 114,958 women) in 1984.

Francis Brown, a golf addict, was tried in the courts at Banff, Scotland, for stealing two golf balls, found guilty and hanged in 1637.

Fewest putts by a man for 18 holes was 15, by professional Richard Stanwood, Caldwell, Idaho in 1976, and by amateur Ed Drysdale, Cheraw, Colorado in 1985.

Fewest putts by a woman for 18 holes was 17, by professional Joan Joyce, Stratford, Connecticut in 1982 and 19 by amateur Beverly Whitaker, Pasadena, California.

Fastest round of golf—seventy-seven players completed the 18-hole, 6502-yard Kern City course, California, in 10 minutes, 30 seconds, on August 24, 1984 using only one ball and scoring an 80!

There are approximately 85 golf club manufacturers in the United States.

The most aces shot in one year is 33 by Scott Palmer, a feat accomplished between June 5, 1983—May 31, 1984, all on holes between 130 and 350 yards in length in San Diego County, California.

The greatest number of holes-in-one reported in a career is 97, by Scott Palmer of San Diego, California who was born in 1958.

The largest green in the world is reputed to be the Par 6, 695-yard fifth hole at International Golf Club, Bolton, Massachusetts, with an area greater than 28,000 square feet. That translates into a square with each side approximately 167 feet.

The lowest score for eighteen holes was scored by English professional, Alfred Edward Smith, who shot a 55 on his home course in 1936.

The first postage stamp in the world that was related to golf was issued by Japan, in 1953. The United States and Great Britain didn't issue one until 1973.

International team matches started with amateurs, England versus Scotland, in 1902. England won 32 holes while Scotland won 25 holes.

India was the first country outside of Great Britain to play golf and that was in 1829.

The lowest score with one club was a recorded score of 70 (2 under par) on the 6,037-yard Lochmere Golf Club course in Cary, North Carolina and shot by Thad Daber of Durham, North Carolina in 1987.

The longest officially recorded long drive was accomplished by Jack Hamm of Denver when he drove the ball 406 yards in 1986. This was done in an official PGA long driving contest in which the drive had to land in a fairway only 40 feet wide.

Byron Nelson holds the record for winning the most tournaments (18) in a single season. Additionally, of those 18, he won 11 consecutively, also a record. Feat accomplished in 1945.

Longest Putt—Bob Cook (United States) sank a putt measured at 140 feet 2 3/4 inches on the eighteenth at St. Andrews, Scotland in a professional-amateur tournament on October 1, 1976.

The highest golf course in the world is the Tuctu Golf Club in Morococha, Peru, which is 14,335 feet above sea level at its lowest point.

The lowest golf course in the world is Furnace Creek Golf Course, Death Valley, California, at approximately 178 feet below sea level.

Golf is a $20-billion-a-year industry worldwide while in the United States it is a $5.2 billion industry. Golf equipment sold had total sales in 1988 of $3.1 billion.

Golf is the game of choice for 80% of the CEOs of major corporations according to a survey taken in 1988.

In 1989, purse money on the PGA Tour was approximately $42 million.

There are approximately 23.4 millon golfers in the United States.

There were an estimated 487 million rounds of golf played in the United States in 1989.

In the United States there are approximately 13,626 golf courses, of which 8,300 or so are private or semi-private.

Japan has an estimated 11,300,000 golfers while only having 1,558 golf courses. You think your golf course is crowded!

The census of world golf indicates that there are close to 50,000,000 golfers in the world who play on a total of 24,000 golf facilities.

Based upon 1984 and 1988 figures golf is played in 76 countries of the world. In Russia there are apparently no golf courses.

The five countries with the most golfers, and the golf facilities that are available are as follows:

United States	23,400,000	13,626
Japan	11,300,000	1,558
Canada	2,200,000	1,796
England	596,000	1,300
Korea	500,000	43

Oldest golf club in the world is reported to be the "Honourable Company of Edinburgh Golfers" which came into existence in 1744.

The state of Florida has more golf courses (1,000) than any other state in the United States. Additionally, there are reportedly 45 courses currently under construction. The 1,000 golf courses, if laid out in a straight line, would be approximately 3,500 miles long.

Which of the following golf balls have you played with during your years of playing the game? Be careful, the golf balls you say you have used could possibly date you!!

feathery
gutty
gutta-percha
Acme
Ocobo
Silvertown
Glory Dimple
Green Circle
Black Circle
Spalding Dot
Baby Dimple
Haskell Whiz
Red Honor
Red Dot
Maxfli
Colonel
Star Challenger
Why Not
Triumph
Clackheaton
Colonel Click
Bullet Honor
Kro-Flite
Silver King
Vardon Flyer
Hot Dog
Rocket
Slazenger
Status

Eagle
Titliest - Balata
Excalibur ELT 416
Top Flite Plus
Hogan
Pinnacle
Wilson Pro Staff
Ultra
Condor
Golden Ram Laser 392
Bullet
Dunlop Red Circle
Molitor
Bridgestone Precept
Tour Edition
Ram Tour
Dunlop XLT-15
MacGregor Master
Flying Lady
Spalding Elite
Golden Ram
Ping
Titliest DT
Maxfli Tour LTD MD
Pinnacle Gold
Maxfli Master
Top Flite XL
Maxfli DDH III
Top Flite II

The following names are the ancient precursors of the modern day set of golf clubs. How many clubs do you have in your golf bag? Imagine playing a round of golf with just the following:

Brassie—the term for what today would be a 2 wood
Spoon—term for what today would be a 3 wood
Cleek—term for what today would be a 2 or 3 iron
Mashie—ancient lofted club equivalent to a 5 iron today
Mashie Niblick—ancient lofted club equivalent to a 7 iron
Niblick—ancient lofted club equivalent to a 9 iron

The oldest recorded playing foursome had a cumulative age of 361, and was comprised of Maurice Pease, 98, Joseph Hooker, 94, Richardson Bronson, 85, and Stanley Hart Sr., the youngster at 84.

Most consecutive one-putt greens—18, by Rick Coverdale, Baltimore, Maryland in 1958, and by Johnny Pallot, Coral Gables, Florida in 1981.

Fastest round of golf on foot was 28 minutes, 9 seconds, accomplished by Gary Wright on the 6,039-yard Tewantin-Noosa Golf Club, Queensland, Australia, in 1980.

Most recorded golf courses played in a lifetime is 3,625 by Ralph Kennedy, New York City, New York.

The bouncing ball record is held by Mark Mooney of Hummelstown, Pennsylvania, who bounced a ball off the face of his pitching wedge 1,764 times.

Golf ball sales around the world total approximately 500 million dollars or over 20 million dozen golf balls!

Women comprise 23% of the total golfing population; however, 41% of new golfers are women.

THE SIDE GAMES WE PLAY & WAGER

GAMES THREE

The games that follow in this chapter for the most part include a higher level of betting or wagering than the games previously described. In some cases the games allow for a change of partners on every hole, or a new bet on every hole. Additionally, some of the games allow a player or team to decide their own fate by having a player pick a partner or by having a team bid on what their total score will be for a hole.

In some of the following games strategy is definitely a factor not only in how one plays a hole but in how one bets that hole. You will also find some interesting formats for both threesome and fivesome play. With all the bets, and potential press bets, coupled with any garbarge games that might be played, an accountant in the group would prove beneficial to determine who wins and who loses money at the end of the round!

Remember, you are out to have fun, so if you can't lose it, don't bet it!

CENTER or RIGHT

After deciding the order of tee-off for the foursome, everyone tees off, and teams are decided by the two drives that are closest to the center or the two drives that are furthest to the right. The two teams then play for two points a hole: one point for low score and one point for low total score. If there is a tie on the hole then the teams stay the same for the next hole. If there is no tie, then the player designated as the second player on the first hole tees off first on the second hole and so on until the fifth hole when, providing there have been no ties, the player who teed off first on the first hole tees off first again. After playing the round everyone's points are totaled and the difference between player points determines who pays whom and how much is owed.

ONE-HALF AGGREGATE SCORE

This is a game played when there are only three players and the players are of reasonably equal playing ability. The game is broken up into six-hole matches with one player for the first six holes playing against one-half of the aggregate score of the two other players. As an example, if player A and player B are teamed for the first six holes and score a four and a five on the first hole, then player C has to beat four and one-half on the first hole in order to win. The same format used for the next five holes.

The second six-hole match starts on hole seven with player A playing against one-half the aggregate score of player B and player C on holes 7 thru 12. The third match would therefore cover holes 13 thru 18 using the same format. You

"You can be the greatest iron player in the world, or the greatest putter, but if you can't get the ball in position to use your greatness, you can't win." Ben Hogan on the importance of drives

can play each match for a set amount or you can play that each point won is worth so much money. At the end of the eighteen holes, add everyone's pluses and minuses and the player(s) with the minuses pays the player(s) with the pluses.

FOUR BALL FOURSOME

This is played with two players on a side with each playing their own ball. The low ball of each team counts on each hole with the low ball of the foursome winning that hole. The team that has the most low balls on the most holes wins the match. This is also fun to play when you have two or more foursomes out playing and you play the same format but with the low ball of the foursome counting towards the match with the other foursomes. We play this with each player putting a set wager into the pot and the foursome that has the most low balls on the most holes wins the pot and divides it up among the four players. (See scorecard example 3.0)

LOW BALLS OF FOURSOME

There are no predetermined partners in this game; however, partners are decided by the two players who shoot the two lowest scores on each individual hole. The points that are lost or won are determined by the difference in the total score between the two low balls and the two high balls. For instance, if two players both score fours while the other two players score a five and a six the point differential is three (eight versus eleven). The point value is decided before the start of play. If there is a three-way tie for low ball or if there is a tie for second low ball, no points are earned or lost for that hole.

FIVESOME WHEEL

This fivesome game involves a preselected twosome playing a match against the other three players that form three twosomes. For example, if by ball toss, players D and E are the two closest balls, they become the wheel team and play against players A, B and C. These three players form three twosomes, AB, AC and BC, who each play a separate match against the wheel team of DE. Usually full handicaps are used in this game. However, some play off the low handicap player and have their handicaps adjusted accordingly, with the low handicap player thus playing as a zero. The games that can be played among the four teams vary tremendously, however, the games played most often are: a net best ball low score for the 18 holes, a high-low point game, or regular Nassau with presses when a team is two down. If your team is the wheel, hopefully you are on your game; otherwise it could prove to be an expensive day.

BEST BALL FOURSOME

This game is somewhat similar to the previously described four ball foursome. In this game, however, you require at least two foursomes, one foursome playing against the other. The twist to this game is that each member of the foursome has their score contributing toward the team scores on a minimum of three holes of the eighteen. Whether playing against another foursome or three or four foursomes each team scores their best ball(s) as follows: on the first hole the best ball of the foursome is recorded, then on the second hole the two best balls of the foursome are recorded for a team total, then on the third hole the three best balls are recorded as a team total, then on the fourth hole the team's total score for all four players is recorded as a team total. After the fourth hole, the scoring process is again repeated on the fifth hole, the ninth hole and the thirteenth hole. On the 17th hole only the best ball of the foursome is used for the

"The hardest shot is a Mashie (5 iron) at ninety yards from the green, where the ball has to be played against an oak tree, bounces back into a sand trap, hits a stone, bounces on the green and then rolls into the cup. That shot is so difficult that I have only made it once." Zeppo Marx

FOURBALL FOURSOME

In the example below Players A & B play against Players C & D. In this example players play off B's handicap (handicaps are in parentheses), so Player A gets 2 shots, Player C 1 shot and Player D 2 shots. Handicap holes are circled.

HOLE	1	2	3	4	5	6	7	8	9	Out
Black Tees	422	347	107	598	392	239	454	517	414	3490
Gold Tees	386	336	104	512	361	230	416	474	364	3183
Silver Tees	353	272	67	486	329	188	370	447	350	2862
PAR	4	4	3	5	4	3	4	5	4	36
Handicap	7	15	17	3	11	9	1	5	13	
PLAYER A (25)	5	6	4	7	5	4	⑥	5	7	49
B (23)	6	5	4	6	6	5	6	6	6	50
BEST BALL WIN				1						
PLAYER C (24)	5	5	3	8	5	5	⑥	5	6	48
D (25)	4	5	4	7	6	4	⑤	7	5	47
BEST BALL WIN	1		1				1		1	

INITIALS	10	11	12	13	14	15	16	17	18	In	Tot	Hcp	Net
	362	445	548	324	183	435	169	403	589	3458	6948		
	337	406	509	281	150	413	139	374	564	3173	6356		
	326	377	443	255	95	335	116	349	503	2799	5661		
	4	4	5	4	3	4	3	4	5	36	72		
	16	6	4	12	14	2	18	8	10				
A	5	6	6	4	4	(6)	4	6	7	48	97		
B	4	5	7	5	3	5	5	6	6	46	96		
	1				1						3		
C	6	5	7	4	4	6	4	6	6	48	96		
D	5	7	6	5	4	(6)	4	5	6	48	95		
								1			5		

Scorecard 3.0

As indicated above Players C & D win 5 best ball holes while Players A & B win 3 best ball holes. As a result, Players C & D win 2 points each from their opponents.

team score while on the 18th hole the two best balls of the foursome are used for the team score.

The team that has the lowest total score for the 18 holes is the winner. In the case of one foursome playing against another, each player on the winning team wins whatever the predetermined bet or wager was. When there are more than two foursomes playing, you can then have an individual bet with the other foursomes or you can agree to every player putting a dollar or five dollars into the pot with the winning foursome splitting the pot among themselves.

This game can also be played so that everyone gets their full handicap and takes the handicap strokes where they fall on the scorecard. Providing that pros, or amateur pros, or all low handicappers are not playing, a team score in the range of 180-190 is a good score, especially if using gross scores.

AVERAGE SCORE

This game is played with partners playing against the rest of the field using their individual gross scores as a means to determine their team score. Both partners play each hole and then average their total score to determine their team score. After completing their round they then subtract one-half of their combined handicap from their eighteen-hole total to determine their net score. Half strokes count as whole strokes after totaling. You might wager against other teams based upon the difference in the team net scores or you might even arrange Nassau bets based on your average scores.

EVERY THREE HOLES

This is a good game for five players. It is like a Nassau, but you change partners every three holes so that one player

"Golferswhotalkfastswingfast." Bob Toski, Golf Digest '82

always has two other players as individual partners. In essence there are three two-player teams, each playing against the other. When I've played this game, we either play best ball or low total score wins the hole. Another variation I've played has automatic presses when you go one down. A team might go one up on the first hole and then lose the second hole and thereby be even on the first bet, one down on the second bet. Then, if they lose the third hole they will end up one down on the original bet, two down on the second bet, and one down on the third bet because of the second automatic press that took effect after the second hole.

After three holes you throw balls in the air to decide who will be partners for the next three holes. The player who did not have two individual partners now becomes the swing player. After every player has had the chance to be the swing player, allow the player who is losing the most the option to be the swing player for the last three holes. Add up everyone's pluses and minuses to decide who pays whom. At times we have found that because of all the matches, automatic presses, and the fact that we also play skins, sandies and proxies, an accounting nightmare results requiring all five players to push a pencil to determine who has won and who has lost.

ECLECTIC

This game can be played either individually or with two-player teams. The game itself can be played in two different manners. The first method involves the selection of nine holes drawn out of a hat or cup after everyone has completed play with the nine holes consisting of two par threes, two par fives and five par fours. The winner is the player with the lowest best ball score or total team score for those nine holes.

The other method of playing this game uses the best or lowest score achieved by a player or team on two of the par threes, two of the par fives, and five of the par fours out of the eighteen holes played.

In this game, using either method, usually one-half of a player's handicap is used.

AUTOMATICS

The only time I have heard of this being played is between golfers with low handicaps. Basically this is a game in which a new bet starts on every hole regardless of the results on the first hole. Even if you tie the first hole it still means that going off the second tee you are even and zero depending on how you do on that hole. If perchance you win the second hole that means you go to the third tee plus one, plus one and zero. After nine holes in a match like this the players should have a minimum of eight matches besides any other bets, wages or garbarge being played. In a game like automatics you need a lot of scorecard and a lot of lead in the pencil.

The game becomes even more complex from a scoring standpoint if you play both individual as well as team automatics. In this event I strongly encourage engaging the services of a certified public accountant who can keep the columns of bets straight with the debits and credits going into the proper player column, as well as providing a reasonable accounting of who won and who lost at the end of the match!

EIGHTY-ONE or NINES

When you are short a player and only have a threesome, this is a good game. Each hole has a total point value of nine and nine times nine holes is 81 and thus the name of the game. Players either play heads up (with no

"If you keep shooting par at them, they all crack sooner or later." Bobby Jones

ACCORDING TO MY C.P.A.,
YOU LOST BIGTIME!

handicap) or with full handicap, taking shots where they fall on the scorecard. The winner of the hole is the player with the best score, who is awarded five points; the next best score gets three points, and one point for the high score. In the case of two players tying for best score, split the first and second points so that they each get four points. If all three players tie for low then each player gets three points. When two players tie for high score, split the second and third points so that each gets two points.

Prior to playing, decide how much each point is worth. The point value can be anything that you and the others decide. The total points at the end of nine holes should be 81, and the same for the back nine, so that the total of all players' points at the end of eighteen holes should be 162. Totaling the points for all players determines who pays whom, with the low-point total player paying both the other players based on the point differential. The second high-point player also pays the high-point player based on the point differential. (See scorecard example 3.1)

TWELVES

This is a game similar to Eighty-One or Nines, but played by a foursome with each individual playing against the others in the foursome. It can be played by low handicappers as a gross score game or by mixed level handicappers as a net score game. In Twelves, points are won on each hole based upon performance, with the point breakdown on each hole as follows: the low score wins six points, the second low score wins four points, the third low score wins two points, while the high score on the hole gets no points. In case of a tie for low score between two players, they would split the

"It's a compromise of what your ego wants you to do, what experience tells you to do, and what your nerves let you do."
Bruce Crampton, on Tournament Golf

EIGHTY-ONE or NINES

Players A, B & C get full handicaps, with handicap holes circled, and the points won on each hole indicated below each player's score.

HOLE	1	2	3	4	5	6	7	8	9	Out
Black Tees	422	347	107	598	392	239	454	517	414	3490
Gold Tees	386	336	104	512	361	230	416	474	364	3183
Silver Tees	353	272	67	486	329	188	370	447	350	2862
PAR	4	4	3	5	4	3	4	5	4	36
Handicap	7	15	17	3	11	9	1	5	13	
PLAYER A (12)	⑤	4	3	⑥	⑤	③	④	⑤	4	39
PTS.	2	4	3	2	3	4	5	3	4	30
B (14)	⑤	5	3	⑤	⑥	⑤	⑤	⑤	⑤	44
PTS.	2	1	3	5	1	1	2	3	4	22
C (11)	④	4	3	⑥	④	③	⑤	⑤	5	39
PTS.	5	4	3	2	5	4	2	3	1	29

INITIALS	10	11	12	13	14	15	16	17	18	In	Tot	Hcp	Net
	362	445	548	324	183	435	169	403	589	3458	6948		
	337	406	509	281	150	413	139	374	564	3173	6356		
	326	377	443	255	95	335	116	349	503	2799	5661		
	4	4	5	4	3	4	3	4	5	36	72		
	16	6	4	12	14	2	18	8	10				
A	5	(5)	(7)	(3)	3	(4)	4	(6)	(6)	43	82		
	2	2	1	5	2	4	3	1	3	23	53		
B	5	(4)	(5)	(6)	(3)	(5)	4	(4)	(6)	42	86		
	2	5	5	2	5	1	3	3	3	29	51		
C	4	(5)	(6)	5	3	(4)	4	(3)	(6)	40	79		
	5	2	3	2	2	4	3	5	3	29	58		

Scorecard 3.1

In the above example, Player C wins 58 total points and would win 7 points from Player B that had 51 total points, win 5 points from Player A that had 53 total points. Note that all Player points add up to 81 on the front side and 81 on the back side to total 162 points.

points for low and second low score so they would each win five points. In the case of a three-way tie for low score, each player would win four points, and in the case of a four-way tie each player would win three points. Ties for second low score or for high score would be handled in a similar fashion, with the available points being split equally among the players. The total of all player points on each of the nine holes should total 108.

Some players like to play this game because they do not have to depend upon a partner and can concentrate on their own game. However, some also play this game in conjunction with some of the garbage games or a Nassau.

The winner in Twelves is the player with the most points at the end of the round. This player is paid by the other players an amount equal to the difference in their point totals times whatever each point is worth. As an example, you are playing for .10 cents, and player A had 59 points, player B 54 points, player C 64 points, and player D 39 points. Therefore player A, B, and D all pay player C the following: player C 64 points – player A 59 points = 5 points × .10 = $.50; player C 64 points – player B 54 points = 10 points × .10 = $1.00; player C 64 points – player D 39 points = 25 points × .10 = $2.50.

Points for the entire game should total 216. (See scorecard example 3.2)

SIXTEENS

In this foursome game each individual plays against the others in a fashion similar to the game Twelves. As in Twelves, this game can be played by both low and high handicappers as a gross or net score game. In Sixteens, points are won on each hole based upon the following performance: low score wins seven points, second low score wins five points, third low score wins three points and the high score on the hole wins one point.

Ties are handled in a similar fashion to Twelves, with the points equally split among the players who tie. As an example, if three players tie for low score, then each player wins five points and the high score wins one point; or, if two players tie for low score and two players tie for high score, the low score players each win six points while the high score players each win two points.

As with Twelves, this game can be played in conjunction with some of the garbage games or even a Nassau match. The winner in Sixteens is the player at the end of the round with the highest point total. The winner is then paid by the other players based on point differentials times the value of each point. The same method is used to pay both second and third high point players. In Sixteens the total of all player points should equal 144 for each nine holes, or 288 points for the 18-hole round. As a check, remember that on each hole the total of all player points won should equal 16.

LAS VEGAS

This game is usually played by one twosome against another twosome, and the individual scores of each twosome are compared. In comparing scores, the low ball followed by the other score determines points won or lost. A twosome that scores two fours versus their opponents' four and five wins one point. A forty-five (4-5) minus a forty-four (4-4) is equal to one. If the score of a twosome is forty-four (4-4) versus a fifty-six (5-6), then the low twosome wins twelve points. This game gets dangerous because if the winning twosome wins by scoring a birdie, then the points being

"Bob, you can't always be playing well when it counts. You'll never win golf tournaments until you learn to score well when you're playing badly." Jim Barnes, teaching professional giving advice to a young Bobby Jones

TWELVES

A game which is similar to Eighty-One or Nines, but played by a foursome with points earned as follows: low score 6 points, 2nd low score 4 points, 3rd low score 2 points and the high scorer earning no points. In this example players play with full handicaps, with handicap holes being circled, and points won, if any, below the player's score.

HOLE	1	2	3	4	5	6	7	8	9	Out
Black Tees	422	347	107	598	392	239	454	517	414	3490
Gold Tees	386	336	104	512	361	230	416	474	364	3183
Silver Tees	353	272	67	486	329	188	370	447	350	2862
PAR	4	4	3	5	4	3	4	5	4	36
Handicap	7	15	17	3	11	9	1	5	13	
PLAYER A (12)	⑤	4	3	⑥	⑤	③	④	⑤	4	39
	3	4	4	3	4	5	6	4	3	36
B (14)	⑤	5	3	⑤	⑥	⑤	⑤	⑤	⑤	44
	3	0	4	6	1	0	2	4	3	23
C (11)	④	4	3	⑥	④	③	⑤	⑤	5	39
	6	4	4	3	6	5	2	4	0	34
D (15)	⑥	⑤	4	⑦	⑥	④	⑤	⑥	④	47
	0	4	0	0	1	2	2	0	6	15

INITIALS	10	11	12	13	14	15	16	17	18	In	Tot	Hcp	Net
	362	445	548	324	183	435	169	403	589	3458	6948		
	337	406	509	281	150	413	139	374	564	3173	6356		
	326	377	443	255	95	335	116	349	503	2799	5661		
	4	4	5	4	3	4	3	4	5	36	72		
	16	6	1	12	14	2	18	8	10				
A	5	5	7	3	3	4	4	6	6	43	82		
	2	2	0	6	1	5	4	1	2	23	59	TOTAL	PTS.
B	5	4	5	6	3	5	4	4	6	42	86		
	2	6	6	1	5	1	4	4	2	31	54	TOTAL	PTS.
C	4	5	6	5	3	4	4	3	6	40	79		
	6	2	3	1	1	5	4	6	2	30	64	TOTAL	PTS.
D	5	5	6	5	3	5	5	6	5	45	92		
	2	2	3	4	5	1	0	1	6	24	39	TOTAL	PTS.

Scorecard 3.2

As indicated above, Player C wins with a high point total of 64 points and therefore wins from Player A (64−59) 5 points, from Player B (64−54) 10 points, and from Player D (64−39) 25 points.

LAS VEGAS

A game with team AB playing against team CD with teams playing even. The scoring is from team AB's standpoint in regard to team points won/lost.

HOLE	1	2	3	4	5	6	7	8	9	Out
Black Tees	422	347	107	598	392	239	454	517	414	3490
Gold Tees	386	336	104	512	361	230	416	474	364	3183
Silver Tees	353	272	67	486	329	188	370	447	350	2862
PAR	4	4	3	5	4	3	4	5	4	36
Handicap	7	15	17	3	11	9	1	5	13	
PLAYER A (12)	5	4	3	6	5	3	4	5	4	
B (14)	5	5	3	5	6	5	5	5	5	
	55	45	33	56	56	35	45	55	45	
PLAYER C (11)	4	4	3	6	4	3	5	5	5	
D (15)	6	5	4	7	6	4	5	6	4	
	46	45	34	67	46	34	55	56	45	
TEAM PTS. WON/LOST	-9	–	+1	+11	-10	-1	+10	+1	–	+3
CUMULATIVE TOTAL		-9	-8	+3	-7	-8	+2	+3	+3	+3

84

INITIALS	10	11	12	13	14	15	16	17	18	In	Tot	Hcp	Net
	362	445	548	324	183	435	169	403	589	3458	6948		
	337	406	509	281	150	413	139	374	564	3173	6356		
	326	377	443	255	95	335	116	349	503	2799	5661		
	4	4	5	4	3	4	3	4	5	36	72		
	16	6	4	12	14	2	18	8	10				
A	5	5	7	3	3	4	4	6	6				
B	5	4	5	6	3	5	4	4	6				
	55	45	57	36	33	45	44	46	66				
C	4	5	6	5	3	4	4	3	6				
D	5	5	6	5	3	5	5	6	5				
	45	55	66	55	33	45	45	36	56				
	-10	+10	+9	+38	-	-	+1	-20	-10	+18			
	-10	-	+9	+47	+47	+47	+48	+28	+18	+18	+21		

Scorecard 3.3

Team AB in the above example wins the front side plus 3 and wins the back side plus 18, mainly due to the birdie by Player A on hole #13, which doubled their point winnings on that hole. Team AB wins from team CD a total of 21 points for the 18 holes.

played for are doubled on that hole. For instance, if one team scores a birdie three and a par four (3-4) versus a par four and a bogey five (4-5), then the twosome having the birdie wins a total of twenty-two points ($45 - 34 = 11 \times 2 = 22$). In this game birdies result in a doubling of the points while an eagle results in a tripling of the points. This is definitely a game that can have some amazing swings in winning and losing. (See scorecard example 3.3)

LAS VEGAS, AZ

Another game in which one twosome plays against another. In this format of Las Vegas the scores of each twosome are multiplied and then compared. The difference determines what the high score pays the low score. As an example, if one twosome scores a four and a five their score (4×5) is 20, while their opponents score a five and a five, and their score (5×5) is 25. The differential in this case is five (25 minus 20) and the twosome that scored the 25 loses five points, while the twosome that scored the 20 wins five points. As another example, let's say that one twosome scores fours for a total of 16, while their opponents score a four and a seven for a total of 28. The team that had the 28 loses twelve points each (28 minus 16) and the team that had the 16 wins twelve points each.

One of the players who plays this game is in the insurance business and plays with a "stop loss," which limits the high score on any hole for any player to a maximum of a triple bogey. In this game, as in others, you decide beforehand the value of each point. Also, points lost or won apply to each player of the twosome. Some play that in the case of a twosome that wins the low score total with a birdie, the points that are won are doubled on that hole. To determine who wins and who loses, add up all the pluses and minuses, and the twosome with plus points wins their points times the predetermined value of each point. (See scorecard example 3.4)

HAWK—WOLF—CAPTAINS

This is played with a foursome, in which the first player to tee off becomes the hawk. Each player becomes the hawk on subsequent holes until the fifth hole, when the player who was the hawk on the first hole again becomes the hawk. After everyone has teed off the hawk picks his partner from among the other three players. Naturally the hawk picks the player having the safest and best drive. The hawk and the partner must then beat their opponents by best ball. If they don't, they lose, or if there is a tie then there is no blood and neither team wins. The hawk, however, can decide to play a hole without a partner, and play against the other three players. In this case the hawk must beat the best ball of the other three players. When the hawk goes it alone then all bets are doubled, and if the hawk does lose, the hawk pays each of the other three players double the bet.

This game can be played using full handicaps, which can result in some decision-making by the hawk, especially when deciding to take a partner who gets a shot. Since you will have two holes left after every player has been the hawk four times, the player that has lost the most bets gets to be the hawk for holes 17 and 18. As I have found out many times, the two best drives of a hole do not necessarily guarantee that the hawk team will have the best ball. I have seen some amazing birdies made out of the rough to win the best ball. There was also the case of a player hitting a shot out of bounds off the tee but still shooting a bogey five to win the best ball. The bet value in this game is determined before the start of play and remains the same for each hole.

"The job of a finishing hole is as clearly defined as that of a dance hall bouncer. It has to maintain order, clear out the amateurs, and preserve the dignity of the game." Jim Murray, Golf Magazine '83

LAS VEGAS, AZ

Game with team AB playing against team CD with teams playing even. The scoring is from team AB's standpoint in regard to points won or lost. Remember, in this game twosome scores are multiplied to result in a total score versus that of the other twosome.

HOLE	1	2	3	4	5	6	7	8	9	Out
Black Tees	422	347	107	598	392	239	454	517	414	3490
Gold Tees	386	336	104	512	361	230	416	474	364	3183
Silver Tees	353	272	67	486	329	188	370	447	350	2862
PAR	4	4	3	5	4	3	4	5	4	36
Handicap	7	15	17	3	11	9	1	5	13	
PLAYER A (12)	5	4	3	6	5	3	4	5	4	
PLAYER B (14)	5	5	3	5	6	5	5	5	5	
	25	20	9	30	30	15	20	25	20	
PLAYER C (11)	4	4	3	6	4	3	5	5	5	
PLAYER D (15)	6	5	4	7	6	4	5	6	4	
	24	20	12	42	24	12	25	30	20	
TEAM POINTS										
WON/LOST	-1	-	+3	+12	-6	-3	+5	+5	-	+15

INITIALS	10	11	12	13	14	15	16	17	18	In	Tot	Hcp	Net
	362	445	548	324	183	435	169	403	589	3458	6948		
	337	406	509	281	150	413	139	374	564	3173	6356		
	326	377	443	255	95	335	116	349	503	2799	5661		
	4	4	5	4	3	4	3	4	5	36	72		
	16	6	4	12	14	2	18	8	10				
A	5	5	7	3	3	4	4	6	6				
B	5	4	5	6	3	5	4	4	6				
	25	20	35	18	9	20	16	24	36				
C	4	5	6	5	3	4	4	3	6				
D	5	5	6	5	3	5	5	6	5				
	20	25	36	25	9	20	20	18	30				
	-5	+5	+1	+14	-	-	+4	-12	-6	+1	+16		

Scorecard 3.4

In the above game team AB wins a total of 16 points from team CD, 15 points on the front and 1 point on the back. Once again the birdie on hole #13 was a deciding factor in who won and who lost.

WOLF & PIG FIVESOME

In this game, five players decide upon a numerical order, one through five, by throwing golf balls or by flipping a tee. After the order has been established, the player who has been designated number 1 becomes the wolf and tees off first, with the other players following in numerical order. After everyone has teed off the first player to tee off selects a partner from the other four players prior to leaving the tee box. The hole is then played with the first player, who is the wolf, and selected partner playing a net best ball against the other three players. On the second hole the player designated number 2 becomes the wolf and tees off first, followed by players 3, 4, 5 and player number 1. Once again the player who is the wolf selects a partner of choice after all players have teed off. The same format is used on the subsequent holes three, four and five with player number 1 again becoming the wolf on hole number six. Remember that this is a net best ball between the wolf and partner, and that the partner is selected before leaving the tee box.

What about the pig? If the player who is the wolf has a good drive and the other players' drives are in trouble, or out of bounds, then the wolf can decide to play the hole without a partner and play against the other four players. In such an event, which often happens on par threes, the bet is doubled and it is said that the wolf becomes the pig!

In this game, the wolf team either wins or loses one and a half points, and the other three players win or lose one point each. Point totals are tallied at the end of the round, and total pluses should equal total minuses.

THE DOG

This is a threesome game, using full handicaps, comprised of six parts and the earning of points for each part. The six parts are: two hind legs, two front paws, one tail, and one head, with each point worth one dollar. Parts and points

are won or lost only when a player shoots a score without being tied or beaten. In this game two tie all tie.

As an example, if player A shoots a par on the first hole without being tied or beaten then player A earns a point and has one hind leg. If player A also shoots a par on the second hole, and wins that hole, then player A now has two points and two hind legs. If on the third hole player A is tied by player C, then there are no points or parts won or lost. If on the fourth hole player B shoots a par then player B earns one point and now has one hind leg. Player A, however, with two points and two hind legs, loses one of the hind legs and goes into the fifth hole with two points and one hind leg. On the fifth hole player C shoots a par and therefore earns a point and one hind leg. Player A and B both lose their hind legs. Going into the sixth hole player A has two points but no parts, player B has one point and no parts, while player C has one point and one hind leg. If player C comes into the 18th hole having five parts of the dog and seven points and shoots a par on the 18th, and wins the hole, player C is said to have won the dog. Player C, having won the dog and having earned eight points, wins from each of the other players twice the point total. If player C had been tied on the 18th and had a high point total of seven, then the other players would have each paid player C seven dollars. If two players tie in parts at the end of 18 holes, then the player with the most points wins. In summary, parts and points are only earned when a player shoots a par or wins a hole without being tied. Two tie all tie, and no parts or points are won or lost. If another player shoots a par while others have a part or parts of the dog, those players each lose one part of the dog, but do not lose their previously earned points. The player who ends the round with the most parts is the winner, and is paid by each of the others the total earned points. If a player wins the dog, having all six parts, then the winning points are doubled. If a player wins the dog early in the round, start another game for the remainder of the holes.

BRIDGE

This game, played with partners, is a little more complex than some of the other games in that it requires both planning and strategy by the partners.

The game involves a team bidding what they believe their aggregate score on a hole will be. The opposing team can accept this bid or can double the bet believing that the bid will not be achieved. The opposing team can also underbid the original bid, which means that they now have to achieve the aggregate score of their bid. In this situation the team that was underbid can also double the bet. Another variable is that the team that has been doubled can redouble the bet.

As an example, let's say that you and your partner start the action on the par four first hole and that you are playing for a dollar a point. On the first tee you and your partner both feel that you can par the hole so you bid an eight. The bid is accepted by the other team and you and your partner play the hole in an effort to score an aggregate total of eight or better. If your team achieves a score of eight, you both win a point, or one dollar. If your team achieves a score of seven you would both win two points, or two dollars.

If, however, you end up with an aggregate score over your bid, you and your partner lose a point for each shot that exceeds your bid. If for example, using the above bid of eight, you and your partner score a four and a six for a total of ten, two shots over your bid, you both lose two points, or two dollars.

As another example, let's say the second hole is a tough par five and therefore your team bids an eleven. The opposing

"Real Golfers have two handicaps: one for braggin' and one for betting." Bob Irons, Red Bluff

94

team thinks about doubling you since they know that your partner never plays this hole well, but instead they decide to take the bid away from you by bidding ten. Your team then doubles the bet, since you don't deem your opponents capable of achieving their bid. Your opponents, however, are confident they can, so they redouble the bet. In this situation each point is now worth four dollars.

In the above example if the bidding team shot a four and a five for an aggregate score of nine, versus their ten bid, the team would win two points, with each player winning eight dollars since the original bet was doubled and then redoubled.

In this game, bids alternate, regardless of who wins the bid. Some play this game with the bets automatically doubling in the event that: 1) the team that takes the bid not only achieves their bid, but does so with both individual scores being lower than their two opponents' scores; 2) the team that takes the bid achieves it but does so with a birdie or an eagle.

In this game, sometimes bidding to not take the bid is most important. Also, using bidding strategy to get your opponents to bid themselves into a tough position can be fun, and allows you to escalate the betting by doubling. Thinking and strategy on how you are going to bid is different on every hole.

BACKGAMMON or DOUBLE

This game is similar to Bridge, the big difference being the potential for betting runs through the entire hole. The game ends once everyone has putted out. The game can be

"The number one thing in trouble is: don't get into more trouble!" Dave Stockton, Golf Magazine '77

played individually or in teams. Low total score wins in this game; however, the betting can be distracting.

Using a team format as an example, this is how it's played: the team that starts off is said to have the "cube" and states that they will score a total of nine on the hole which is a par four. The other team accepts the bid and everyone then tees off. The team that made the bid apparently has hit one of their drives out of bounds or into the deep rough. As a result of the apparent difficulty in achieving a nine for the hole, the other team doubles the first team, which means the bet is doubled. At this point the first team can either accept the doubling and play on, or they can admit that they can't achieve a nine and concede the bet on this hole. Let's say that this team accepts the double and upon arriving at the ball in the rough, they find it not only in bounds, but also having a good lie and an open shot to the green. As a result, they double the bet again. The second team can either concede the bet on this hole or accept the bet and the match proceeds. After everyone has hit their shots it appears that the first team has hit one ball over the green and the other into a trap while the other team has left a ball short of the green and another on the green, but with a putt that is in three-putt range. The second team, seeing themselves in no trouble, then doubles the bet again. The first team can again concede the match and not accept the double and lose a total of four points each or continue. In this case they continue and accept the double, which is now eight points. The first team put their third shots on the green with one ball five feet from the cup and the other two feet from the cup. The second team leaves both their balls short of the hole by ten and fifteen feet. The first team, believing that they can sink at least one of their putts and believing that the other team won't, doubles the match. The second team thinks they can sink one of their putts and they know that both the other players are poor putters so they accept the double, which means they are now playing for sixteen points. As it turns out the first team misses both their putts while the second team sinks one of theirs to end up with low total and win sixteen points each on this hole, which is only the first hole of eighteen. If everyone had missed their putts, then they would have tied and there would have been no blood. If one player gets a shot on a hole this can really influence the course of betting, as well as the strategy.

THREESOME HAWK

With only three players the Hawk game can still be played by having the missing fourth player become a bogey score for every hole played. The format is the same as in a four-player game. As in the four-player game, decide upon an order of play, and then after everyone has hit their drives, the first player, who is the hawk, selects a partner prior to leaving the tee box. In this game the hawk has a choice between the other two players or a bogey score for the hole as a partner. In this game low net score wins the hole. In the case of a tie neither team wins or loses and the player who was designated number two becomes the Hawk on the next tee box. This game also allows a player to go it alone on a par three or possibly on a tough par four or five, especially when the other two players have driven into trouble off the tee. However, remember that when a player does decide to go it alone the bets or point values are doubled for that particular hole.

SIX, SIX & SIX or RANSOM

This is a two-player team game that is broken into three separate six-hole matches. The format for this game is as follows: on the first six holes the best ball of the twosome counts, for the next six holes the players play alternate shots

"A great golf hole is one which puts a question mark into the player's mind when he arrives on the tee to play it."
Mackenzie Ross, Golf Course Architect

until the ball is holed out with the low twosome score on each hole winning that hole, and for the final six holes the aggregate score, or total score, of the twosome is used. In the above game betting can be on an individual hole basis, which means that a total of eighteen points can be won. Another way to bet this game is to have each six-hole format equal one bet so that a total of only three bets can be won or lost. This game can be played with full handicaps; if there is not a large discrepancy in handicaps, the teams can play even.

REJECT or WIPE OUT

This game can prove to be frustrating and/or funny depending upon whether you or your team is the replayee. In this game, played either individually or on a four-ball basis, each player or team has the right to have their opponent replay four shots during the course of the round. Therefore, if you are playing four-ball teams the opponents have the right to have both you and your partner replay four shots, with your team having the same right. In this game you or your partner might hit a great drive, cutting a dogleg leaving only a short chip shot to the green, or possibly you or your partner hit a career shot to the green leaving the ball only inches from the cup for a sure birdie or eagle, or even possibly you or your partner have sunk a long birdie putt, only to have your opponents, or golfing friend, call for a replay. Sometimes all of the above occur and you can therefore appreciate that this game can be both frustrating as well as funny depending upon your perspective. The betting in this game can be either a straight medal or a match game, or even a Nassau.

99

THE SIDE GAMES WE PLAY & WAGER

GAMES FOUR

Other games we play are more of a golf outing, club function or tournament nature. These types of games vary extensively in format but for the most part are fun to play. I have undoubtedly not included all the different types of golf formats available, but I believe that what is included will provide variety enough to plan games for a year or more.

With the following games you can have a prize for the winning team or group, or you can arrange to have your team play against another team or be brave and bet the rest of the field that your team will beat them. The wagering and betting is sometimes just as much fun as the playing. So on to the games—again?

DROP OUT

Utilizing full handicap and taking shots as they fall on the scorecard, the players play against par. The winner is the player who can play the most holes in straight succession without losing to par. If a player shoots a bogey on the first hole and doesn't get a shot, then he is out of the match. This format is used until there is only one player left who has not lost a hole to par. This is most often used in conjunction with other types of games or bets. In Drop Out the winner wins the pot into which all players have put a predetermined amount of money. If you have a large field of players you might even pay out to three or four places. It is surprising how many low handicappers bogey the first hole or first few holes because they are not sufficiently warmed up. Low handicappers do not always win in this game.

THROW OUT GAME or TOURNEY

In this game a player may throw out three worst holes so that only fifteen holes are counted in determining score. This game is usually played with full handicap, thus resulting in a net fifteen hole score. You usually bet this game based on the total fifteen hole net score of each player. You may even arrange a "robin" game so that you can play three five-hole matches.

SCOTCH TWOSOME

In this game two players alternately hit the same ball until it is holed out. If, for example, player A tees off on the first hole, a par four, then player B hits the second shot from wherever player A's drive came to rest. If however, player A hits his ball out of bounds, then player B retees hitting three. Continuing the example and providing that player A has not

"The way I putted, I must've been reading the greens in Spanish and putting them in English." Homero Blancas, when asked to comment on his putting in the '70 Masters.

hit out of bounds, player B hits the second shot and hits the green. Player A then putts and misses, leaving the ball short of the hole. Player B then putts and sinks the putt for a team score of a par four. Going to the second tee, player A tees off since player B hit the last shot, or putted last. This is strictly a game in which the players hit or putt the ball on every other shot or putt regardless of what the player before has done.

SCOTCH FOURSOME

This game is played exactly the same as a Scotch Twosome, but there are four players. After selecting the order of play for each player, player A tees off with player B hitting next, and so on through C and D. If the ball has not been holed out after player D, then player A hits or putts again. The same order is maintained throughout the eighteen holes of play. If player C happens to hole out, then on the next tee player D gets to tee off, followed by player A, and so on. It's a game that keeps the entire team together throughout the eighteen holes of play, and it can and does result in a lot of kidding and verbal harassment among team players. "Nice guy—you have only left me a 30-foot putt!" Or, "Thanks a lot, now I have to hit a shot over water." Or possibly, "That's great, what do I do with a fried egg lie in the sand trap—I've never seen a lie like that, much less know how to hit it!"

FLAG TOURNAMENT or TOMBSTONE TOURNAMENT

In this contest each player is provided with a small flag with their name attached to the flagstick or on the flag itself. Using full handicaps, each player plays until they have used the number of strokes equaling par plus handicap, and at this point the player's flag is planted. If a player still has strokes

"Golf is not a game you can rush. For every stroke you try to force out of her, she is going to extract two strokes in return." Dave Hill, Teed Off '77

left after eighteen holes, then that player continues to play until all shots have been used, which in some cases might extend to two extra holes. The winner of this type of play is the player who plants the flag at the farthest point around the course. In the case of playing a Tombstone Tournament, instead of flags each player should have a marker in the shape of a tombstone. Additionally, each tombstone, when planted, should have some type of epitaph such as "Here John West expired," or, "If it weren't for Dick Smith's duck hook, he would have survived longer," or, "Mary Higgins died here because of three putts!"

CHICAGO SYSTEM

This is a game that can also be played in conjunction with other matches or bets. In this game each player is given a predetermined point quota which is based on their handicap, as indicated below. Points are scored for all players regardless of handicap as follows: bogey one point, par two points, birdie four points, eagle eight points. The player whose point total for eighteen holes most exceeds their point quota wins. If no one exceeds their point quota then the winner is the player who comes closest. Remember that in this game points are determined strictly on gross score, not on net score. Winner wins the pot, or, if you have a large number of players, you can pay out to third or fourth place.

Another way to play this game is that the low point player of the foursome pays off the three players who have more points, and payoff is based upon whatever point value was

"Caddies are a breed of their own. If you shoot a 66, they say, 'Man, we shot a sixty-six!' But go out and shoot a 77 and they say, 'Hell, he shot seventy-seven!' " Lee Trevino, They Call Me Super Mex, 1982

predetermined times the differential in point totals. Besides the low point player paying off, the player in third place also pays off the second place and first place players, and the second place point player pays off the player with the most points. The payoffs are all based on the point differentials among the players.

HCP	QUOTA	HCP	QUOTA	HCP	QUOTA	HCP	QUOTA
1	38	10	29	19	20	28	11
2	37	11	28	20	19	29	10
3	36	12	27	21	18	30	9
4	35	13	26	22	17	31	8
5	34	14	25	23	16	32	7
6	33	15	24	24	15	33	6
7	32	16	23	25	14	34	5
8	31	17	22	26	13	35	4
9	30	18	21	27	12	36	3

CALLAWAY SYSTEM

18 HOLE REGULATION COURSE: This is a handicap system devised by Lionel Callaway, the former head pro, Pinehurst, North Carolina. This particular system allows for the handicapping of players who do not have an established handicap, a system generally associated with large outings. In this system a player's handicap is determined after the completion of the round. The gross score of the player determines the handicap adjustment by eliminating a worst hole or worst holes and subtracting the adjustment from the player's gross score.

The table that follows indicates the worst-hole deductions that are allowed, and an adjustment based upon gross score. If, for instance, a player shot a gross score of 100 the table indicates that that player can deduct the three worst holes that were shot. In this example, the player's three worst holes were a nine, and two eights which adds up to a handicap of 25, plus the indicated adjustment of plus two results in a total handicap of 27. Therefore, this player's net score would be

100 minus 27 which equals 73. The following notes should also be observed when using this system.

1. Maximum handicap allowed is 50.
2. No hole should be scored at more than two times its par.
3. Unless you are using a Shotgun format, the seventeenth and eighteenth holes should never be deducted.
4. Half strokes count as a whole stroke.
5. In case of ties and no scorecard playoff, the lower handicap or adjustment should be given preference.

		Score			Deductions for Handicap
		70	71	72	Scratch and adjustment
73	74	75			1/2 worst hole and adjustment
76	77	78	79	80	1 worst hole and adjustment
81	82	83	84	85	1 1/2 worst holes and adjustment
86	87	88	89	90	2 worst holes and adjustment
91	92	93	94	95	2 1/2 worst holes and adjustment
96	97	98	99	100	3 worst holes and adjustment
101	102	103	104	105	3 1/2 worst holes and adjustment
106	107	108	109	110	4 worst holes and adjustment

Regarding Pine Valley Golf Club, Cleminton, N.J., "tell me, do you chaps actually play this hole—or just photograph it?" Eustace Storey, British Amateur, on his first look at the second hole.

111	112	113	114	115	4 1/2 worst holes and adjustment
116	117	118	119	120	5 worst holes and adjustment
121	122	123	124	125	5 1/2 worst holes and adjustment
126	127	128	129	130	6 worst holes and adjustment

Adjustment

−2	−1	0	+1	+2	deduct or add to handicap

MODIFIED CALLAWAY SYSTEM

18 HOLE PAR THREES: Since par three golf courses have different scoring requirements than a regulation eighteen-hole course, the Callaway System has been adapted to account for this difference using the format below.

1. Half strokes count as the next highest whole number.
2. Unless using a Shotgun start, do not deduct scores for the seventeenth and eighteenth holes.
3. In the case of ties where a scorecard playoff is not used, the low handicap takes preference.

Score	Deduct
54 — below	Scratch, no adjustment
55 to 57	1/2 worst hole
58 to 62	1 worst hole
63 to 67	1 1/2 worst holes
68 to 72	2 worst holes
73 to 77	2 1/2 worst holes
78 to 82	3 worst holes
83 to 87	3 1/2 worst holes
88 to 92	4 worst holes
93 to 97	4 1/2 worst holes
98 to 102	5 worst holes
103 to 107	5 1/2 worst holes
108 to 110	6 worst holes

TIN WHISTLE PLAY or PAR/BOGEY PLAY

This is another game involving points that are awarded based upon a player's score and is somewhat similar in nature to a Stableford or Hogan game. In this game however, points are awarded based upon the following: one point for each hole that is made in one over par, three points for each hole that is parred, and five points for each hole in which a birdie is scored. This game is played with full handicap so that a hole in which a player has a stroke would count as a birdie if the player scored a par on the hole and would therefore earn five points. The player who has the most points at the end of the round wins the pot or the point differential between the other players times the value, as decided earlier, of each point. This game is reputed to have originated with some Pinehurst golfers known as the Tin Whistles.

TWO PLAYER SCRAMBLE

This involves two players as a team, both playing their own shots and then continually selecting the best ball of the two, including putts, until the ball is holed out. As an example, player A and player B both tee off on the first hole which is a par four. Player A hooks the ball into the rough while player B hits a drive into the middle of the fairway a good distance off the tee. Selecting player B's drive, both player A and player B hit their second shots to the green from the spot of player B's drive, and again select the best shot from which to proceed. In our example, player B pushes the shot into the greenside sand trap while player A has hit a shot fifteen feet from the pin. Selecting player A's ball, both players putt from where player A's ball is. Player A putts first and putts the ball three feet past the pin. Player B putts and leaves the putt just

"The best swing we have is our practice swing. Unfortunately we never use it." Ken Venturi, PGA Magazine 1990

a few inches short of the hole. Selecting player B's putt, player B then putts out sinking the putt for a team score of par four. If player B had sunk the putt, and not left it short, after player A had putted then the team score would have been a birdie three. In this game, if a player inadvertently taps in a putt before the partner has had a chance to putt, then the hole is considered to be completed, and the partner does not get to putt.

FOUR PLAYER SCRAMBLE

This game is just like a two-player scramble, but involves four players. Each player tees off and the best drive is selected and then all players hit their second shots from within twelve inches of the best drive. This format is used on each series of shots or putts, always selecting the best shot or putt of the four, until the ball is holed out. Remember that if the first, second or third putter has not holed out and by force of habit taps in the putt after missing the original putt, the remaining players do not putt, as the hole is considered to be completed. So if a putt is missed, regardless of how close it is, mark it until all have putted.

As an equalizer in this type of game, it is common to mix both high and low handicappers together on the same team. I have played in games that require that each player's drive be used on at least three or four holes of the eighteen. With this in mind, it is sometimes better to use a high handicapper's drive that is only 175 yards off the tee, but in the fairway, rather than a low handicapper's drive that is 275 yards off the tee. Strategy in selecting shots, especially drives, can be crucial to how the team scores.

"As of this writing, there are approximately 2450 reasons why a person hits a rotten shot and more are being discovered every day." Jay Cronley, Playboy '81

TWO BALL FOURSOME

In this game two players are a team and use only one ball, and partners alternate in playing the shots. One partner drives from all the odd-numbered tees and the other partner drives from all the even-numbered tees regardless of which partner hit the last shot or made the last putt.

If there is not a large discrepancy in handicaps among the four players, this game can be played as a straight gross score. If, however, there is a major difference in handicaps, then usually one-half of the combined handicaps is used to provide some parity between the teams. This game can be played by two twosomes or by an entire field of players that could be comprised of 72 twosomes. If you are playing another twosome you can arrange almost any type of bet, whether a medal game, match game or even a Nassau game. If there are more than two twosomes you can arrange a bet with the other twosomes, or everyone can agree that each team puts into the common pot a set amount of money with the winning twosome taking the pot. If there are more than eight twosomes then you can split the pot and pay out as many places as you decide.

THE WHEEL

Using full handicaps this game is played in a best-ball twosome format. With a minimum of sixteen players, each player can select from one up to a maximum of three other players as partners and pay a set amount of money for each partner selected into a common pot or kitty. At the end of eighteen holes the players then compare their scorecards with their partners to determine the lowest net score for each hole. The player who has the lowest score wins the pot and any other money that might have been bet by the other players. Once again, if there is a large field it is common to pay out as many places as is agreed upon before play.

CRIER'S MATCH

This game can be either a straight match in which you play hole by hole with or without handicap, or you play a medal match in which you compare your total score, gross or net, to your competitor's. Each player gets to pick out their two or possibly three worst holes compared to par, and revert these scores back to par. If you are playing teams then the above format is still used with the team's worst two or three holes reverting back to par and then deciding who has won the match. This type of play can have some interesting results. If you play with someone who is always saying "If I hadn't shot this or that on those two holes I would have beaten you," well, this is a game in which you can give them a chance to beat you.

LONG AND SHORT MATCH

Called this for lack of a better name, since some players have better long games than short games, and vice versa, this game combines the ability of both types of players. For instance, you might be straight and long off the tee and hit your irons the same way, but once you get around the green or have to hit a pitch shot, you have the touch of a gorilla! However, you have another player who, if their life depended upon it, could not drive or hit their irons, but amazingly, has a great touch around the greens. In this type of play you would drive and hit all the long irons while your partner would hit all the approach shots and do all the putting. The type of bet you make in this type of game often depends upon your faith in your partner.

ODD AND EVEN MATCH

This is played twosome against twosome, or as many as want to bet. In this game one player of the team plays all the even holes, and the partner plays all the odd holes. Usually only one-half of the combined handicap is utilized to determine the net score of each twosome, with low net score winning. This game can be played at the same time you are playing other games, such as a Nassau. Just decide whose score will be used on the odd and even holes and then play your regular game with everyone playing all eighteen holes.

BEST BALL CHAPMAN or PINEHURST

In this best-ball game (involving teams of two players), both partners drive and then both hit their second shots and then decide which ball to play for the third shot regardless of whether it is an iron shot or a putt. The player whose second shot was not selected is the player to hit the third shot, with the partners then alternating every shot until the ball is holed out. This format is followed for the entire round of golf. If you play this game it is usually played with one-half of the team's total handicap and, depending upon the type of game you are playing, the handicap can be deducted from the gross score or the handicap strokes can be taken where they fall on the scorecard.

BEST BALL GREENSOME

In this format two partners both drive and then select the best drive from which to hit the second shot. The drive that is not selected is the partner who hits the second shot, and the partners alternate hitting the shots until the ball is holed out. This same format is used on all subsequent holes. One-half of the team's total handicap is used to derive a net score or, if involved in a match format, the handicap strokes are applied where they fall on the scorecard.

BEST BALL GRUESOME

In this game one twosome plays against another twosome; the opposing twosome selects which drive of the

"It's good sportsmanship to not pick up lost golf balls while they are still rolling." Mark Twain

other twosome is to be played, naturally choosing the worst drive. Once the drives have been selected each player of the twosome plays out the hole. This game can be played as either the best ball of the twosome or total score of the twosome.

BEST BALL BLOODSOME

In this twosome game both partners hit their tee shots, and the opponent twosome selects which shot of the two will be played for the second shot. As in Best Ball Gruesome, the opposing twosome naturally selects the worst drive, and the player whose drive was not selected hits the second shot. Play then proceeds with each partner hitting and/or putting alternately until the ball is holed out. In this game the best ball wins the hole.

BEST BALL FENSOME

In this twosome game both partners drive and then select the best drive from which to hit their second shot. However, in the Fensome format one player hits all the second shots on the odd-numbered holes while the other player hits all the second shots on the even-numbered holes, regardless of whose drive was selected. After the second shot has been played the partners then alternate shots or putts until the ball is holed out. One-half the team's total handicap is used to determine a net score or, if in a match format, the handicap strokes are applied where they fall on the scorecard.

BEST BALL RYDER CUP

In this format each team consists of two players with each player driving on either all the odd-numbered holes or the even-numbered holes. The player who does not drive is the player who hits the second shot and the players alternate hitting the shots or putting the ball until it is holed out. This is the format that the pros play, and therefore, it is usually a

format best suited for good players, particularly due to the demands placed upon the player driving the ball.

NO ALIBI EVENT

In this game, instead of deducting a player's handicap at the end of the round, each player is allowed to replay or rehit, during the round, the number of shots that is equal to three-fourths of their handicap. Some play using full handicaps. A stroke that is replayed must be used even if it is worse than the original shot, and it can not be replayed a second time. The replay can also apply to putts. This game can be played individually with the low score winning or with teams playing either a best ball or total score for the twosome or foursome.

SHAMBLE

This is a point game in which a foursome plays as a team to accumulate as many points as possible against the rest of the field. In this game everyone on the team hits a tee shot and then the foursome selects the best drive, and from the spot of the best drive, each player in the foursome hits the second shot and continues to play out the hole. Players in this game use their full handicaps with points earned individually based upon the following: one point for par, two points for a birdie, three points for an eagle, and four points for a double eagle. Points are totaled on each hole for all four players, and the team with the highest point total at the end of the round is the winner. The points that are won are based upon net scores of each individual player, which allows each player to contribute to the game. This is also a game that tends to favor the higher handicap player and with this format, players often find that they are able to shoot scores that are five to ten shots better than they normally do. It is also a game format that brings everyone together as a team with each player pulling for the other.

THE 19TH HOLE

Well, hopefully the games that have been described don't get you into trouble. They have not been intended to, but rather the intention was to provide you the opportunity for more fun, competition and social intercourse while on the course. Remember, we do not play the game for a living and therefore firmly believe that a good part of the game is the company you play with.

Regardless of who buys the drinks or who wins or loses, good company provides the theatre to commiserate about that poor shot, poor round or, on the other hand, reliving and explaining that great shot or score. Enjoy the game and the company you play with.

Finally, I realize that in all likelihood there are other games that people play or variations to the games that have been described that I have not included in this book. That is due to the fact that I have not played them or have not heard about them. If you play a game, or have a variation of a game that has not been described, please drop me a line and let me know about that game.

"Golf is a game of inches. The most important are those between the ears." Arnold Palmer

THE UNITED STATES GOLF ASSOCIATION and THE ROYAL AND ANCIENT GOLF CLUB OF ST. ANDREWS, SCOTLAND

Policy on Gambling

The Definition of an Amateur Golfer provides that an amateur golfer is one who plays the game as a non-remunerative or non-profit-making sport. When gambling motives are introduced, problems can arise which threaten the integrity of the game.

The USGA does not object to participation in wagering among individual golfers or teams of golfers when participation in the wagering is limited to the players, the players may only wager on themselves or their teams, the sole source of all money won by players is advanced by the players and the primary purpose is the playing of the game for enjoyment.

The distinction between playing for prize money and gambling is essential to the validity of the Rules of Amateur Status. The following constitute golf wagering and not playing for prize money. 1.Participation in wagering among individual golfers. 2.Participation in wagering among teams.

Organized amateur events open to the general golfing public and designed and promoted to create cash prizes are not approved by the USGA. Golfers participating in such events without irrevocably waiving their right to cash prizes are deemed by the USGA to be playing for prize money.

The USGA is opposed to and urges its Member Clubs, all golf associations and all other sponsors of golf competitions to prohibit types of gambling such as: (1) Calcuttas, (2) other auction pools, (3) para-mutuals and (4) any other forms of gambling organized for general participation or permitting participants to bet on someone other than themselves or their teams.

The Association may deny amateur status, entry in USGA Championships and membership on USGA teams for international competitions to players whose activities in connection with golf gambling, whether organized or individual, are considered by the USGA to be contrary to the best interests of golf.

INDEX